OFF THE
HOOK

First published in February 2011

© Text and pictures - Rosie Barham

© Illustrations - Kate Barham

© Design - Mpress (media) Ltd

© Cover picture - Paul Moulder

ISBN NUMBER 978-0-9567015-5-8

Unit Four, Ashton Gate, Harold Hill, Romford, RM3 8UF

Designed and published by m press (Media) LTD.

For: Thomas George, Mia Rose, William Edward (Win) and Holly Louise, the next generation - and David and Kate, Simon and Lucy, without whom...

Thanks to: Cliff and Paul Moulder, Elton Murphy, Terry Doe, Tim Paisley...also without whom...

Line drawings by Kate Barham.

Photographs courtesy of: Leon Roskilly, Dave Barham, Terry Doe, Simon Barham and Jim Midgely.

Edited, and occasionally enhanced, by Terry Doe.

OFF THE HOOK
CONTENTS

OFF THE HOOK

PREFACE

How revealing the benefit of hindsight. 'The Fishing Widow's Guide' was intended as a cautionary tale to FWs everywhere and written when I was in the thick of living with a husband and two sons who were obsessed with all things piscatorial. At the time, our circle of friends was gripped by the same fever and my life seemed to revolve around all aspects and disciplines of the sport.

Sadly, a few years ago, the relationship between the Chief Angler and I deteriorated beyond repair. The reasons did not include the fact that he spent nearly all of his leisure time near water; I had no problem with that. I grant you that a contributory factor was his total preoccupation with large amounts of liquid, but the only things swimming in it were slices of lemon and slivers of ice.

Be that as it may, looking back on my life spent as a fishing widow and mother of two angling sons, I don't

Early morning mist, and mates. My idea of heaven.

regret any of the 'fishing' bits of it. It was such fun; hard work at times, but it paid off in the end. My two sons left home and moved away; one to Peterborough, to become editor of popular sea fishing magazines, the other to Portsmouth where he carp fishes regularly as a way of unwinding from his stressful and demanding job. David and Simon have partners who I am proud to call my daughters-in-law. They are both fully qualified fishing widows already, and cope enormously well.

What follows are reflections of how it was, and how it is now. I have caught fish of my own and I'd never have believed that possible had it been predicted ten years ago. So there is hope for fishing widows, providing they keep a sense of humour and go with the flow. Never, ever say, 'it's only a game', though.

OFF THE HOOK

INTRODUCTION

Through the keyhole

Who lives in a house like this? I could just imagine Loyd Grossman wandering about proclaiming, in our fishing household. He'd have had no trouble working out the predominant interest.

Front garden: Stone 'Cutty Sark' in between patio pots, and a marble-effect carp amid petunia border.

Entrance hall: Overflowing with rod racks, nets, umbrellas, grown up romper suits, tackle boxes, bivvies - two or three of everything - and bait freezer.

Front Room: Fourteen pictures of fish, mostly carp. One framed box of nautical knots, three shelves of fishing books and videos, antique reels artistically arranged in between Capo di Monte figurines.

Back Room: Framed fishing photos, three more shelves of angling books and mountains of fishing magazines.

Morning room: Another bait freezer, and fishing shelves that filled a wide alcove and contained every item of tackle you could possibly require at any given time or season.

Kitchen: Fish recipe books, bait flavourings cupboard, stockpot for cooking boilies, boilie rolling table and associated equipment. Three small Chinese figures holding fishing rods with carp attached - and that was just downstairs. I dare not list the items in the boys' bedrooms; I'd be here all day.

When a friend brought his young sons on a first visit, they were entranced and as good as gold all day; there was no bad behaviour through boredom. I was usually careful about who I allowed into the house. To qualify for admittance, any guests had to have a sense of humour and be agile enough to negotiate their way past, and sometimes over, all the fishing gear, but my friend telephoned me the next day with reassuring words.

The boys' enthusiastic verdict on our humble, Victorian end terrace would have done justice to a stately home. 'Fantastic house!' they'd chorused. 'So much to look at. Every room's got something interesting in it. Auntie Rosie didn't mind if we sorted out our tackle boxes on the carpets, and there were fishing mags to read while on the toilet. Brilliant!'

They were junior anglers, of course, grown now into fine young men with obsessions intact.

Me and a perch painted by the CA. No one ever took photos of me because I never held fish. For a long time, this was as close as I got.

It's a matter of time

If you're a fishing widow, and/or mother to assorted anglers, you may not notice your own leisure hours diminishing through no fault of your own. There will be small but time-consuming tasks that must be performed, usually with the utmost urgency, on behalf of your family because they are at work, school, or just fishing.

One day you may realise that one of the reasons you no longer have the time to read a daily newspaper until the events in it are history, is that you are involved in angling indirectly, whether you like it or not. You may even begin to suffer from stress-related ailments before you cotton on. Those headaches need not be attributed to the cheese baguette, chocolate torte, and glass of red wine you had for lunch.

It isn't deliberate. They don't go out of their way to prevent you from having a few moments to yourself. It's just that they are preoccupied with their main interest and consequently, either leave things until the last minute or forget them altogether. This results in panic-stricken telephone calls to the one who they know is willing and able to get them out of trouble.

On one occasion, I received an agitated phone call from number one son who begged me to rush to Woolworth without delay, in order to purchase a couple of packets of balloons, 'good quality ones, please, the cheap ones burst on contact.'
"Contact with what?" I asked.
Had he taken no notice whatsoever during my frequent and explicit lectures on the use of condoms? I'd even mentioned the possible emergency uses of cling film and elastic bands. He didn't take me seriously, at least, I hope not, and knew that I just needed to drive a point home, so to speak. It turned out that the balloons were to be used as marker floats in the pursuit of blue shark and porbeagle. I nearly bought a couple of those party popper thingys while I was at it, for celebration purposes when, or more likely if, one was actually caught.

The most irritating aspect of living with anglers, personally speaking, was this gradual erosion of spare time. I could see my life being hacked away in delicate 30-minute chunks purely because of a few well-chosen and very often incomprehensible words.

"Could you just pop up to the tackle shop and get me a packet of hooks for tomorrow?" This was always late on Friday afternoons. "Write this down and then give me a ring when you get home so that I know you've got the right ones."

When I did call them back, offering reassurance and the detailed description of my purchase demanded by my anglers just in case I'd got it wrong again, there would be something else they'd forgotten and I'd have to trudge all the way back to the tackle shop to buy the indispensable item. Well, all right, I didn't *have* to do anything, but for the sake of a quiet life, a hassle-free weekend, or just a few hours in an argument-free zone, I found that a little errand-running was a wise move.

Many other popular and regularly used phrases make up a considerable proportion of an angler's vocabulary. Here's a classic:

"As I drove past the fishmonger's this morning on the way to the station, I saw them unloading a ton or two of fresh, bright-eyed herring. Be a sport. Go and buy us a stone." This request was closely followed by, "Could you bag 'em up separately, once you get them home? Two in each bag should do nicely before you stack them in the freezer. Make sure you do it gently, though, don't hurl them in and squash 'em."

If you agree to this request, not only will you have to go to the fishmonger and queue up for half an hour with a multitude of senior citizens who have also noticed the influx of herring on their way back from getting their pensions, but you must also visit a hardware shop.

Almost certainly and inconveniently, you will have exhausted your usual vast stock of freezer bags the night before and will have nothing in which to wrap your bounty. This store is bound to be at the opposite end of the shopping centre to the fishmonger, I'll put money on it, and it'll probably be seriously raining. When you eventually arrive home, the freezer will have to be reorganised to receive a large amount of fresh fish and the whole exercise can take a couple of hours.

Having to get out of bed in the early hours of the morning when my body and soul were at their lowest ebb was something to which I became accustomed many years ago. As I got older, though, it seemed to be much more of an effort, and it wasn't just a matter of dropping off my anglers at the wharf. I had to wait until they were sure that they were going to cast off, what with the force 5 and all, coupled with the dodgy forecast. Unfortunately, the meteorologists don't always get it wrong.

To be fair, they didn't ask me to wait but I found that it was a good idea because I was caught out on more than one occasion. There were times when I'd just crawled back into a lukewarm bed, only to receive a telephone call to go back and pick them up because the skipper had flatly refused to risk his boat, and therefore his livelihood, for the sake of a couple of whiting with a death wish.

Rarely, if it was a 'late' tide, the 'stop me and fry one' café on the wharf would have opened for business. Then, while they ate, drank and made merry, I'd be allowed to drift off into a half-forgotten and delicious dream in the company of Mark Knopfler and a certain amount of Cadbury, before being rudely awakened and brought back sharply into stark, groaning reality at 6am.

Carp anglers may need a tray of eggs at short notice and 'it will save time' (whose?) if you are the one who goes out to get them. Fresh eggs are vital for boilie-making, and you will be instructed to purchase the very freshest, 'born in a barn' ones. Everything remotely connected with bait making must be of superior quality. We ate the supermarket eggs for breakfast, while the carp enjoyed 'run about' eggs from mobile hens.

A coarse angler may telephone late on a Friday afternoon with an urgent request for maggots.
"There's a box in the garden," he might say. "Only, I've just remembered that I didn't empty out the stale ones last weekend, but you can do that before you take it to the tackle shop, can't you?"

No. I couldn't. There was no way that I would open a box that might contain maggots in chrysalis mode.

There are several stages to their metamorphosis, I know, but I could have been bombarded with bluebottles and I spent enough time avoiding them in the house; they still got spilled after a couple of decades of nagging my anglers to be more careful. I wasn't going to leave myself vulnerable to attack.

If this happens to you, here's a tip. As a substitute container, a large 'I Can't Believe It's Not Butter' tub will hold just about a pint. If you want to live to see your grandchildren grow up, don't leave the lid on without first punching a few air-holes in it because the maggots will otherwise suffocate, and it will be your fault if they have lost their wriggling ability by the time they arrive at a water's edge.

This is also the reason for ensuring that a pot of maggots, left in readiness in the garden in winter (as against your fridge in summer) is in a sheltered place. If it rains, water gets in through the little holes in the lid and if they all drown you will be in big trouble. 'What a fuss! They would have bloody drowned tomorrow, anyway,' is not a wise riposte to a grieving angler.

Then there is the enigma of fishing line around a vacuum roller to cope with. I managed to destroy at least a dozen vacuum cleaners while I was living with anglers. One of the pitfalls of living in a fishing household is the higher than average demise of domestic appliances. Neighbours had the same washing machines, vacuums, and food mixers for 20-odd years; not me. I had to replace everything with such monotonous regularity that the electrical showroom bloke thought I'd got the hots for him.

Every time a new vacuum entered the house, I vowed that this time I would be more careful. I'd forego the excitement that a cleaning session could produce purely because I never knew what I was going to pick up next, and which rhythm accompaniment would ensue. I even grovelled on carpets pre-vacuum, trying to retrieve small items of tackle that had embedded into the shag pile. I did that just once, though.

I tried them all; uprights, spheres and cylinders. I even purchased one expensive variety that was

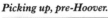

Picking up, pre-Hoover.

supposed to be everlasting. It actually lasted three weeks before I had to rush it to the vacuum cleaner equivalent of Accident and Emergency. A certain manufacturer insists that their machines are so durable and well made that even under the most extreme circumstances no bits of debris can possibly infiltrate the motor compartment. I bought one of these. It lasted until about a week after the extended warranty had run out when a hoarded collection of very small weights, even smaller hooks and mini boilies made of concrete became too much for its innards and it gave up the ghost.

Why is it, when you vac' up fishing line by mistake, that you can't just grab an end and pull it off again? The brushes revolve in the same direction so logic, even the little that I can muster, dictates that I should have been able to solve the problem with ease. When I did find an end to pull, it was always part of a huge bird's nest, which only unravelled about a foot at a time. I knew from plenty of experience that this would need a sharp knife, a complete dismantling job and at least half an hour of precious time wasted.

Did I cut out the middleman and go for the knife straight away, then? Of course I didn't. I'd stand there for a good ten minutes, pulling and tugging, knowing full well that I was flogging a dead horse. The penny dropped eventually and I did start unscrewing things but I never learned to take the thing apart and leave the bits in order for reassembly. Every time, there were a few pieces left over.

If anyone is interested, I still have a boxful of spare parts somewhere for various makes of cleaner.

The next time I vacuumed, the whole exercise started all over again, because I couldn't see fishing line six feet away. I only wore specs for reading and walking about with them on made me feel sick. It seemed a bit extravagant, somehow, to fork out 60 quid for another pair of glasses just so I could see six feet in front of me, downwards. Mind you, when I work out what I must have spent on vacuum cleaners in the past, a special pair of Hoovering specs might have been an investment.

The way in which hooks become embedded in a carpet is a complete mystery. They can't be disentangled, however much you tug, and the culprit is never found. The protestations of wide-eyed innocence that accompany a denial when you accuse can be quite entertaining, but you know that sooner or later you'll have to bow to the inevitable, get down on all fours and snip away at the shag pile with a pair of nail scissors. The latest best seller, meanwhile, beckons temptingly from an armchair where you could be relaxing if only you didn't live with anglers.

Small but quite interesting, injuries all inflicted indirectly (and I'd like to believe but I can't be absolutely sure, unintentionally), by my menfolk took time to repair; time which could have been far better used. Weights that fall off the top of an upright freezer or a high windowsill can cause damage to an unsuspecting fishing widow standing below. Dropped from a medium height they hurt much more than their size dictates they should. Just a 2oz bomb causes a bruise far in excess of expectations.

Then there are the extra-curricular kitchen visits. 'It might be nice to take a chilli out on the boat tomorrow, just to give the lads a treat. I don't suppose you could knock one up this afternoon?' (Friday again, late morning.) My own fault, I know, but pride would not allow me to make it from a couple of pounds of minced beef and a packet mix. I'm still famous for my chilli.

I'd have to go to the shops, which meant a supermarket complete with checkout queue because my friendly local butcher always closed at lunchtime on a Friday so that he could go off fishing for the weekend. I would rather pick rags than embark on any kind of shopping trip, but I needed to buy stewing steak and mince it myself before adding herbs and spices, fresh garlic, peppers and my secret ingredient. Not really, there isn't one. I just made that up.

So 'just knocking one up' involved standing in a hot kitchen for at least an hour until the dish reached my high standard of cuisine. I know what you're thinking. Why did you bother? I knew that once aboard the boat, it was going to be mashed up in a saucepan with the carefully steamed, grain-separate rice and it would look as if someone had already eaten it. I don't know why I bothered, either.

What would we do with our time without these little angling related jobs, though, do you think? We might even tag along and give fishing a go. There is a growing army of female anglers, some of whom started angling by doing just that. They're still in the minority, though, it's definitely a male-dominated pastime. Maybe that's why my anglers did their best to keep me occupied, so that they could escape from me for days at a time. They knew that when everything had been organised and they were packed, ready to go, I'd be too knackered to join them.

CHAPTER ONE

JANUARY FROSTS

An ice touch

You would imagine that a severe frost would stop them fishing, wouldn't you? You'd be wrong. Any normal human being given extreme weather conditions would prefer to stay tucked up indoors in front of leaping flames, accompanied by a red-hot lover and a bottle of plonk or an historical novel and a large Cadbury. Not your average angler, it seems.

If a frost is so prolonged that rivers, lakes, and reservoirs freeze over, then a freshwater fisherman is, for obvious reasons, confined to barracks. I've seen pike anglers, fully grown and usually bearded, near to tears when a hard frost has prevented them from baptising their Christmas presents. The degree of disappointment can be acute and has the strange effect of producing grunted responses to attempts at conversation, until this issue can be overcome. However, a mere thin coating of ice is not enough to discourage sea anglers.

You might see blue bits on the weatherman's map and think, given the predicted cold snap, that at last you will have your angler all to yourself. Do not even begin to consider removing the skimpy, sheer, black nightie, kept for a special occasion (note the singular, here), from the cryogenic tank. Or, for those far from the first flush of romance, don't think for a second that there's a fair chance of getting those odd jobs done around the house. Your angler, who spotted the blue bits before you did, will open an outer door, sniff the crispness in the air and utter the immortal words, "Smell that! That's cod weather, that is!"

There follows a complete monopoly of the telephone while a number of vital calls are made. The most important one is to their friendly charter-boat skipper who is usually as obsessive and dedicated to fishing as his customers. Having booked a place on the boat and been reassured that bait will be provided, and informed of the time of kick-off, they begin to pack their chosen vehicle to the brim with cold protection devices. Within a matter of hours, flasks of hot soup, extra socks, waterproof romper suits and assorted bottles of spirit are stowed carefully before they follow their own dragon's breath into the Arctic wastes and head toward a stretch of coastline in search of cod.

As this ritual will more than likely occur week after week, you may find that you have latent talents. It's fairly easy to hang wallpaper; the few lumps and bubbles that will inevitably appear, because we can't all be Linda Barker, can be smoothed to the lower part of a wall and then hidden by heavy furniture. Better still is painting a wall while clad in old clothing and rubber gloves. This can be very satisfying, particularly if you imagine your absent anglers' bodies in place of the anaglypta.

They will come back some 12 hours later, make a cursory remark or two about your inadequate attempts at DIY, tell you that you've missed a bit on your newly-emulsioned work of art wall and then have the effrontery to tell you that there were no fish to be caught. They'll offer hallucinatory tales of 30-foot waves, icebergs, hands stuck fast to boat rails and the terror experienced while having to expose certain parts of themselves in order to urinate over the side of the boat in sub-zero temperatures. Twelve anglers and a skipper, awash with hot soup, chilled beer and warming tea, serviced only by a small, chemical commode make this a necessary and regular, activity.

Hallucinatory tales.

Before the advent of insulated clothing, the Chief Angler pulled all kinds of stunts in order to keep frostbite at bay. The bathroom sponge, he told me, when accused of theft, was 'only borrowed' early morning and cut in half before being secured, one piece over each ear, by the weight of a balaclava. It seemed to do the trick in that it prevented his ears from freezing solid and dropping into the drink and it had an added advantage, I was told, when eventually the sponge was returned to its proper place. I should now consider myself fortunate that there was a choice of two sponges. How many women could delight in such luxury?

There is no doubt that the excessive amount of alcohol consumed in an effort to keep out the cold grants a certain degree of success in the insulation department. However, the CA (and you can be sure that he wasn't alone in his philosophy) tended to insist that this success was due, solely, to the bathroom sponges. Frequent but traditional rum toddies had nothing to do with it.

Homes from home

Freshwater anglers don't seem to mind the cold, providing the lakes and rivers haven't frozen over completely. Just a few square feet of clear water amid the ice will suffice for a day's sport, and carp anglers have it made. A good quality bivvy can provide a home from home and is surprisingly warm. They also come in handy if there is a power cut, apparently.

David, the eldest, left home some years back, to work for 'Improve Your Sea Angling' magazine in Peterborough, although at the time it didn't feel as if

...if the rivers and lakes haven't frozen over...

he had flown the nest at all. He was home every other weekend with a load of dirty washing, his hand out, and his mouth open. Quite a bit of his fishing gear was still in residence at the family home as a kind of security blanket, but he took the most important items with him so that he could pursue his carp fishing at the weekends when he wasn't working, i.e. sea fishing.

Maybe because they spend many hours camped beside water, carp anglers become accustomed to necessity being the mother of invention. Useful survival techniques can be learned at a lakeside and so, during a prolonged power cut when Dave's all-electric home was without, on a January night with the temperature plummeting to 4° below, he set up his bivvy on the lounge carpet and slept in that. In a thermal sleeping bag and with an occasional cup of tea brewed on a portable, petrol-powered Coleman stove, he was far more comfortable than his neighbours. Very cosy, he said it was, too.

For 20-odd years, I had fitted all the carpets in our house. Fishing widowhood made this an obligatory talent along with other traditionally male tasks like replacing roof tiles, un-bunging drains, digging the vegetable patch, washing the car and so on. You name it; I more than likely did it. The laying of carpets became second nature and I developed a talent for calculating angles. Eventually though, after decades of replacing carpets at yearly intervals, I lost the required motivation so getting someone else to do it seemed a good idea. I paid a young friend to do the job.

Unfortunately, my area calculating ability falls far short of accurate, and because of this handicap I found that I had overestimated the yardage to such a degree that I was left with a number of remnants of a reasonable size. If arranged artistically and stuck down with industrial sticky tape, they would carpet another small room. I telephoned the eldest.

"Dave," I said. "I've got some bits of carpet left over. If you fancy doing a jigsaw puzzle with them, they'd be better than nothing in your threadbare house and it will warm the place up a bit." (It's the middle of winter; are you eating enough? Look after yourself, wear a vest and have you got a clean hanky?)

He was impressed. Grateful beyond the bounds of decency and it was a good few minutes before I understood why. His intention, he informed me, was to cut the carpet to shape and to use it on the floor of his bivvy when he ventured lakeside during the winter months. I should have guessed. He was already taking a duvet and a couple of pillows. Fitted carpet was a natural progression! Along with the cooker, lamps for light and heat, cool box for food, bivvy slippers, miniature, battery operated TV... I was surprised he didn't negotiate for net curtains and a small sofa.

A cautionary tale

I often hear of potentially nasty accidents, near misses, and rarely there are tragic incidents where the foolhardy have succumbed to their fate. It's worth thinking about at this time of the year. Accidents can happen so easily if you're not vigilant. Common sense might be useful, too, on occasions!

A friend of mine had taken his nine-year-old daughter for a 'fun' day out fishing beside a semi-frozen lake. Aided by perseverance and much cursing, he had managed to find sufficient clear water in which to cast, but the rest of the lake and surrounding vegetation was in the grip of a penetrating frost.

Emma didn't mind being there. Fishing with Daddy had the edge over trailing behind Mummy for several exhausting hours; also at Lakeside, as a matter of fact, but the overcrowded, overpriced and, in my opinion, overrated shopping mall, rather that the outdoor version.

Added to the thrill of drinking tea with Daddy and pretending she was an Eskimo princess, was the anticipation that it might actually snow! If she was a good little girl, and stuck it out long enough without complaining that her toes were about to fall off, Emma reasoned, the Fates might smile upon her and let loose the white stuff. Unfortunately, Emma has a low boredom threshold, like most children, and wasn't prepared to sit quietly and watch her daddy lose his temper with the elements.

You can guess the outcome of this story, I'm sure. Emma had been told, 'Don't go near the water,' on bright, sunny summer days, but no one had said, 'Don't try to walk on the water, even if it's frozen solid in the margins and looks as if it'll bear the weight of an elephant.' The kid's nine. While Daddy was looking the other way, she walked, went straight through the ice and into sub-zero watery mud.

Daddy was not pleased. He had to pack up and cart his little treasure home to a warm bath, hot chocolate and Mummy's wrath when she returned home eventually, laden with bargains. Daddy sulked for two days. Mummy got away with spending the best part of Daddy's February salary in the January sales and for days after the event, Emma was spoilt to death by fond grandparents.

When told this small saga, I laughed, but it made me think. I've wandered around frozen lakes on many a winter's day and witnessed the downright stupid things that some anglers do. In the safety of their own homes, they would certainly decry fellow anglers as having no common sense whatsoever but it seems that once beside any volume of water containing fish, their brains are taken over by irrationality and disasters of varying proportions become inevitable.

You will see depressed anglers around many lakes in deep midwinter. Sometimes they huddle together; fingers clasped desperately round steaming mugs of tea. They know there is little chance of a few hours fishing, or even ten minutes, but they hang around anyway. Nobody seems to know why this phenomenon occurs, but my theory is based upon intimate knowledge gained by a lifetime of research into the male ego. They have gone to all the trouble of stowing fishing gear into the car, preparing rigs the night before, steeping bait and so on. If they go home within half an hour of realising they're flogging a dead'un, they will have to admit that they were wrong! Those three little words 'told you so' can strike terror into the heart of a man; so, they go into hover mode.

There are those who do manage to get their end tackle into the icy water, only to have the lines freeze within it. With logic on the back burner, they attempt to Shackleton their way across the lake, prodding forward with a pole to ensure 'safety'. They're on a mission to retrieve a rig that only cost them a couple of quid, and the ice is strong enough to support a prodding pole, but not necessarily the prodder. Give it up! Let the genie of the lake have your precious weight and hook combos. Better that than ending up in A and E with hypothermia, or worse.

I can sympathise to a point. I can't wait for a spring day so that I can get out there, sit in the open air and watch the carp play. I know real carp anglers do this, too. They tell me that it doesn't matter too much if the fish don't want to know; being there is enough, so why venture forth and play 'very silly' near frozen water? It makes more sense to take a flask of hot soup and just sit beside the ice, dreaming of forthcoming and fruitful summer sessions. They're only a few months away!

Take a tip

"What have you been doing all day?" asked the Chief Angler, one cold winter evening. He wasn't interested in the reply but why do men, no matter what their age, always ask as if you've been sitting around doing nothing? They have just been collected from a railway station, eaten a hefty, three-course meal, made their ablutions in a clean bathroom, laid out tomorrow's freshly laundered clothes on a pristine bed and then have the nerve to enquire how many hours you've spent in idleness.

I told him. "I've tidied up the garden," I said, smugly. "Cleared out the shed, bagged up all the rubbish and I've been down to the tip three times. I even got rid of those old bits of carpet that have been lying around on the concrete bit that we laughingly call a patio. There were loads of worms underneath it. Can't imagine what they thought they were doing there, trying to aerate the paving stones, probably."

During this rambling account of my day, he'd had had both eyes on the evening newspaper and one ear tuned into Sport TV, until I uttered the magic word, that is.

"Worms?" his head swivelled round so fast that I wondered if I should call in the Exorcist. "What did you do with them?"

"Nothing," I replied. "What would I do with them? They all made a beeline for the herbaceous border and by the time I came back from the second tip trip, they'd gone."

He went white. "Why didn't you pick 'em up? You could have put them in a box in the 'fridge, couldn't you? Is that too much to ask?"

Well, yes, it is actually. Especially when I'm rapidly losing interest in the job I've started and just want to get it over and done with. The last thing I need is to waste time chasing worms all over the place.

It took him a good few minutes to recover his composure. Next time, I won't mention wriggling things, and there would be a next time; he was already considering the possibility of carpeting over the entire patio area.

Memory

We've all heard the old saying 'owners, after a time, begin to resemble their pets.' Could it be that one of the hazards of habitual carp fishing is that the anglers too, after a time, develop some of the characteristics of fish Like the short-term memory span?

I tried to understand it. I really did, but there were times when the workings of the angling mind left me completely baffled. Like one January weekend when the temperature was fast approaching freezing point, coupled with the kind of dampness in the air that penetrates the bones and, come dusk, turns to severe frost.

Saturday morning dawned and the Chief Angler was up and raring to go. Tackle had been gathered the night before; hot, homemade, chunky soup and assorted sandwiches were hastily prepared for him before take-off so that, at 8am we could trundle merrily toward the club lake with the minimum of delay. I ran an angling taxi for years, the CA never bothered to learn to drive – why would he!

I received a phone call about 3pm from our communal mobile phone. It was mine, and the size of a housebrick; the whole family used it, I just paid the bill.
"Come and pick me up," he pleaded. "I'm really cold and I've not caught anything. I feel terrible."

He looked more than terrible and even after a hot bath, beef stew with dumplings and a couple of hours kip, huddled under a duvet with a hot-water bottle, he was still shivering and told me that he felt chilled to the marrow.

Next morning, he did it again! This time armed with a match rod, which saw the reward of several confused roach, and a legered carp rod that remained inanimate for the duration. I've already made observations on the lack of short-term memory associated with carp anglers, but this time I wondered if there was any memory at all; maybe it wasn't just the carp rod that blanked. Just hours before, he had looked as if he was going to succumb to hypothermia and yet he was prepared to repeat the extreme discomfort just in case a carp might fancy a mid-winter snack. It made no sense at all.

So there you have it. A touch of frost is no deterrent. It all looks very romantic when Chris Yates walks across a winter wonderland at dawn, in his 'Passion For Angling' series. His attempts to sneak up on barbel or carp with more sense than he (they're tucked up in their natural environment, impervious to the elements the deeper they go) makes good viewing, but the reality seems very uncomfortable to me.

Don't knock it until you've tried it

A stereotypical angler exists only in the imagination of those who are not familiar with the sport. There may be the odd lone figure trudging across dew-covered fields, to sit for hour upon solitary hour by a riverbank while in the throes of deep philosophy, but the norm is far more likely to be otherwise. My own experiences with anglers are certainly not of the completely solitary kind. Even when I used to sit with the Chief Angler in a remote swim there were always regular passers-by who would stop for a chat, much to the annoyance of the CA, I have to say, although they brightened up my day no end.

Then there is the other extreme, when a social is organised involving a posse of anglers and their mates; these can be wonderful, shared occasions with people of like mind and a mutual pastime, even when no one expects to catch anything because of the time of year. We attended one of these events, held at a Hampshire water where the management kindly allowed us to bivvy up mob-handed for a Saturday night. This was to be a unique experience for me. I had never, ever before, in my whole life, slept out-of-doors and it was with some trepidation that I agreed to this huge step forward, or possibly backward since there had been several sharp frosts during the week preceding the event.

The day started early. I rose at 4.45 am so that we could arrive at our destination at day-break and was exhausted by the time we had packed the car to bursting point and negotiated the M25 and beyond, through heavy mist, along unlit roads and into darkest Hampshire.

As the mist dispersed and a watery sun took over, I cooked breakfast for what seemed like a multitude, although there were only a few of us; the rest of the party sensibly arrived mid-morning. By lunchtime it was, by comparison with the early frost, like the Costa Brava on the more sociable side of the lake. The CA, preferring solitude, had taken himself off to the other side, of course. He was here for serious fishing and sat in Antarctica quite happily catching small carp. He didn't seem to mind being called Billy No-Mates by his friends from across the water and eventually, he strolled round when he could smell the evening meal cooking – chilli, a large one that I had prepared earlier, and rice.

Soon after supper, everyone wandered up to the bar in the clubhouse for a pint, or several. I settled for half a pint and then a couple of glasses of water having already consumed a considerable amount of the white, fizzy stuff courtesy of one of the anglers. A good way to psyche myself up for a possible uncomfortable night in a bivvy, I reasoned, was to drink a whole magnum almost to myself and eat loads of chocolate. Sufficiently fortified by these forbidden substances, I knew that I'd be able to withstand any amount of unpleasantness. I was never really a drinker so the combination of my earlier over-indulgence with half a pint of something forced the issue and I allowed myself to be led to my bivvy by a dutiful son who was prepared to sacrifice valuable drinking time in order to put his mother to bed. I had borrowed a sleeping bag and a camp bed from a close friend; it has to be a close friend if you're going to fill his sleeping bag with Charlie (it's a perfume – I'm not inhaling anything), and a two-man Titan had already been erected.

This wine is MINE!

The bed had been assembled for me, the sleeping bag arranged neatly and with the top cover turned back. It looked inviting and cosy.

"You'll be all right, Ma," said my eldest. "It's not a bad night, anyway. You want to do it when it's really cold!" (No, Dave, I don't. I'm not sure I want to do it at all, as a matter of fact.) So, because I had no idea what to expect, I prepared myself for a night of misery.

I was awakened around 2.30am, as was the whole lake, by a jubilant shout from Tony Smeets.

"Wake up, everybody!" he yelled. "I've got a 20-pounder, and I think I've broken me thumb!"

Fortunately, he hadn't and such was his elation that I don't think he would have been too worried if he had. I was told, on querulous enquiry as to why we ALL had to wake up just because Tone had caught a fish, that it was 'tradition.'

It was freezing cold, and at two o'clock in the morning, as all you bivvy enthusiasts will already know, it's pitch black. There was a moon, kind of, but there were no street lights or illuminated shop fronts, no light pollution. They told me that was how I was able to see millions of huge stars on a velvet cushion sky. Owls hooted (I have a 'thing' about owls) and I was desperate to catch a glimpse of them but was too scared to get out of the bivvy. You never know what you may encounter while stumbling about in the dark.

Good job I'd stayed put, as I discovered early next morning. Another of our party, a certain Elton 'pretty boy' Murphy, had passed out in the company of Jack Daniels, in a sleeping bag, slap, bang in the middle of the path. He resembled some bizarre, green cocoon and both of us would have had a particularly nasty shock had I ventured out and landed on top of him.

Ice on the roof. Hardcore!

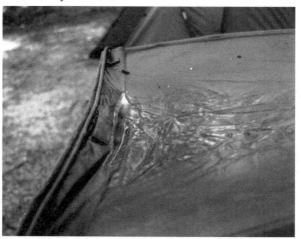

He hadn't intended to sleep on the path, he told me, when I questioned his sanity and pointed out that a bivvy had been provided for his use. He'd got so plastered that he couldn't undo the zip again when he'd 'just got into it for some warmth while I watched me rods for a bit'. His rods had been reeled in and were leaning against a tree, by the way.

Sunday morning, we had a masterclass in tying hair rigs. Mine was the best, they said, but they had just eaten a mountain of breakfast cooked by me, so there would have been big trouble had they said otherwise.

So, despite my forebodings, I enjoyed camping out in the middle of January. It was surprisingly comfortable and I didn't feel the cold. It was a tad off-putting to touch the roof of the bivvy from the inside and hear the tinkle of icicles, but I was dressed warmly and clutching a hot cup of tea so it didn't seem to matter. I'm not quite ready to camp out in a snowstorm yet, but you never know. Give me enough Cava and I might be persuaded.

CHAPTER TWO

FEBRUARY BLIZZARDS

Snow, snow, thick, thick snow

Most winters we get snow. Sometimes, in our sheltered south-eastern corner of England it's just an inch or two at a time but occasionally, and more often elsewhere in Britain, it can settle so thickly that it seems as if a deity has thrown a huge duvet over everything; and still they go fishing.

Imagine the scene. Alongside a wharf, a skipper warms up his boat in readiness for the anticipated arrival of a motley crew who trickle in from the car park, red-eyed, white-hooded and blue-nosed, to stand, staring glumly into a charter boat full to the brim with snow. Snow has stopped falling but had previously fallen so fast and settled so deep that the skipper thought about using his radar to find the engine hatch cover, before they've even cast off.

There's a vital task to be done before the boat can go anywhere. Time for a couple of volunteers to shovel out all the cold stuff before the rest of the party can come aboard. A frantic search made for the ship's shovel reveals nothing. The only explanation, it appears, must be that someone on a previous occasion has made off with it. All that remain in the store are a couple of ancient and wobbly bait-digging forks which are no use as they stand, it'd be like trying to sup soup with a table fork, but dire need being the mother of bright ideas, one of the party has a brain-wave. Every angler carries at least one huge and sturdy carrier bag that contains the makings of breakfasts, lunches, and suppers. These supplies are prematurely violated for rolls of tin foil, carried during the colder months for their most common use in the days before specialised clothing, which was to wrap around frost-bitten toes inside boots. In emergencies, this valuable commodity can be wrapped around the tines of rusty forks in an attempt to manufacture a shovel or two at short notice. The foil drops off, of course, as soon as the forks are plunged into snow and has to be tied on tightly with 50lb breaking strain fishing line before any success can be guaranteed.

So, while the skipper brews up, the deck is eventually cleared, icicles snapped from the gantry and a posse of anglers, exhausted but, by now quite warm, set forth into the wilderness. They're clutching mugs of hot, sweet tea. This old-fashioned and trusted remedy is a reliable treatment for the shock from which they are all suffering. No one expects to be called upon to use a spade during a fishing trip. That's one of the reasons they go fishing in the first place. Other reasons are to avoid holding a paintbrush, wielding a hammer, saw,

They'll do it in any conditions. Leon Roskilly – daft as a brush!

or power drill and driving a car near supermarkets. According to Michael...er...Fish, it's going to be a bright, if extremely crisp, sunny day and they do catch cod so it's all worth while in the end, apparently, but it's certainly not my idea of a good time.

Meanwhile, on the riverbank or at the lake, there's a whole different ball game going on. Freshwater anglers don't seem to mind rod rings icing up. Neither do they object to the possibility of having to emerge from steaming bivvies into the blanketed countryside to deal with a thermostatically challenged tench or shivering roach; most of their expectation is wishful thinking, for it's a rare fish that feeds during extremes of temperature. The best part of the time spent at a water's edge is filled by keeping warm, making endless cups of tea or coffee, heating soup or frying anything that happens to be handy.

Occasionally, either side of the snowstorm there will be a pleasant, if nippy, few days which will produce a decent-sized fish that mistakenly thinks it's mid-April and fancies a snack. These rare days, I'm told, make all the discomfort worthwhile; the most uncomfortable bit being the setting up and putting away of tackle.

One of the things that used to irritate me most about winter angling trips, and I know it's completely illogical and petty, is that after my anglers had left for sea or lake in the early hours of the morning, my

Misguided fishy.

neighbours' paths were virgin snow while ours was a mess of slush and large, boot-shaped footprints. Apart from the fact that it looked untidy, it meant that I would have to pick up a spade and clear it before it froze solid into a lumpy and potentially dangerous surface. I couldn't have returning anglers ending up prostrate and broken-boned, spread-eagled on the path. Mind you, I could have left them there and persuaded the neighbours to believe that they were garden gnomes; they already had fishing rods and pointy hats.

Then there was the searching of the back garden for maggot boxes which had been left outside 'for an airing' because the owner was too lazy to wash them out after the previous week's adventure. The containers became buried under several inches of white stuff and only I knew roughly where they were, because I was in charge of the gardening department, so it was always me who had to grope about in the cold like some mad mountain rescue women to retrieve them. Anxious faces pressed against a conservatory window are a pitiful sight and were always sufficient to spur me on in my search.

The managing of laundry seemed to be more acute in the winter months than in the summer. It should be the other way around. In the summertime we sweat more, take extra showers, change our clothes a couple of times a day, but the problem is, of course, getting things dry. It's easier in hot weather when a machine load or two can be lobbed over a washing line, unnoticed as it dries fairly swiftly in a summer breeze.

In the winter, trying to wash and dry romper suits, numerous wader socks, gloves, sets of underwear, sweaters and jeans, all in triplicate, alongside the ordinary day-to-day washing, was a nightmare that seemed to go on for months.

Once, and only once, I made the mistake of washing 'discarded, dropped to floor on entry to the house' fishing clothes on a winter Saturday. My anglers had intended to walk into their lucky jeans on the way out of the house the following day, but everything was still draped over radiators, too damp to wear. They had to wear unlucky jeans and it was my fault when nothing was caught.

The only consolation to all the hassle of winter fishing is that you don't have to suffer the same discomforts as your menfolk, but can sit quietly in front of a roaring fire, ready to soak up their words of gratitude when they return to hot baths, rib-sticking meals and warm beds – if you're lucky; they're usually too exhausted to speak.

Lake crawls

Sometimes there is a touch of light relief, mid-winter. Now and then, fishing widows are taken out on lake/river crawls on winter weekends. These ventures, often into the unknown, are similar to pub-crawls except that we don't actually get to consume any of the liquid we come into contact with.

These pilgrimages are essential to the well-being of anglers. Without them, the stress levels brought about by the extreme weather conditions could trigger severe emotional crises. When your anglers develop a compulsion to view all the weather forecasts at once, even the American ones on Sky TV because 'sometimes we get their weather', you will know that you've reached a stage where action of some kind must be taken before they go completely off their trolleys. Wrap up warmly, it doesn't take all day, it's well worth the effort and is a small price to pay for mental health, your own included.

We were never alone in our quest. Every lake we visited had its own complement of sad-eyed anglers, huddled together for warmth in the swim nearest the car park. They shook their heads and gazed dolefully at frozen water, tackle nearby just in case February produced an uncharacteristic burst of strong sunshine sufficiently powerful to defrost half an acre of solid ice within minutes.

All were muttering strange incantations under their breath while, to a man and almost in unison, denying all knowledge of the collection of house bricks, scaffolding poles and other large, heavy items that lay accusingly on the surface, where 'some idiot' had tried unsuccessfully to break a float-sized hole in the ice.

There was no response when I asked what would happen if they managed to catch something through a small hole, had they been able to create one.

"You'd never be able to get even a small fish through the hole," I said, "and you'd never land it safely." I could imagine the poor creature swimming round and round in circles for several weeks until a decent thaw set in. The anglers glowered in my direction and gave me those looks that I used to give to my sons when they asked a pertinent but slightly embarrassing question. It served me right; with my experience, I should have realised that when severe withdrawal symptoms set in, logic takes a back seat.

Eventually, we ended up back where we started, at our club water, where one of the lakes had shown signs of thawing in one remote corner, just to make sure that it hadn't re-frozen in our absence. I knew for a fact that the following morning at the crack of dawn, the melted corner would be commandeered by the Chief Angler and his mate while they float fished for six hours in a three-foot radius of clear water before returning home with their psyches intact, oozing tranquillity and bonhomie. Roll on June.

Ducks and dregs

Ducks do not usually begin to target anglers seriously until late spring, when inquisitive, hungry ducklings do their utmost to provoke their victims into childish tantrums, for their entertainment. You can't blame them. It's pretty boring being a duckling I should imagine. There's not much to do except growing and dabbling.

That said, number one son was prey to a couple of drakes in mid-February and accidentally found a way to get his own back. He has witnessed the misery caused to anglers by these feathered maniacs, so he has given me permission to share his secret with you.

Dave and a friend took advantage of an unseasonably fine day out at a local lake where the resident, but confused, duck community evidently thought that spring had sprung and were busy begging for food. He fed them for a while with unsalted peanuts and boilies, following the usual procedure of tempting them away from the casting area and up on to the bank while he cast out, but before he could settle down they soon gobbled up all the bait he was prepared to part with and noisily demanded more.

Dave decided to make himself a coffee, maybe a shot of caffeine would help him to control the impulse to strangle his feathered friends, and out of sheer frustration, he threw them a couple of tablespoonfuls of instant coffee granules. To his amazement, the drakes ate those too, with undisguised enjoyment. Suddenly though, they waddled off to the water's edge where they spent some time drinking and washing their beaks. 'Yik! No sugar!' After half an hour or so they all disappeared and were not seen for the rest of the day, allowing Dave to catch a 22lb 12oz mirror carp. It was well worth the expense of a couple of ounces of coffee, he said, but then he didn't have to buy it in the first place!

Every lake has one

Am I imagining things, or have you also noticed that every stretch of water has one? I've accompanied anglers to various venues over the years and you can bet your last quid that at some point during the session, one'll approach us. I'm talking about the 'it's only me!' individual, loosely based on one of Harry Enfield's characters.

He seems to materialise from nowhere, in any kind of weather; and it's always a man. He appears suddenly out of dense foliage, or thin air, depending on the venue and how much cover is available. He regales us with how things used to be and goes on to argue that all these new-fangled gadgets are not necessary for successful carp angling.

"Bite alarms? Never 'ad them in my day, mate. We made do with a bit of silver paper from a fag packet. Bivvies? We slung a couple of yards of polythene over a bush and as for all that ponceing about with ready-made baits, a few boiled spuds, and a small farmhouse loaf was what we used. We used to catch fish without all this malarkey. You anglers today, you don't know you're born!"

Paradoxically, depending on his mood, he might bang on about the latest gizmos and try to convince us that we'll never catch anything worthwhile unless we have them. Either lecture is usually followed by his 'theory', which makes Einstein's best effort on relativity read like Enid Blyton, and he goes on for what seems like hours. He won't be stopped. You can try ignoring him, telling him that you want to get back to your book, start a conversation with someone else, but none of it makes one iota of difference. He's here to bore the pants off us and won't be satisfied until our eyes glaze over.

"Caught anything?" is always his opening gambit. Lie if you have to but never, ever, give this man a negative response. You'll be lectured at length on the reasons behind your lack of success and receive in-depth instruction on how to remedy your failure. Do not answer if he demands to know what bait you are using. There will be a sharp intake of breath, like plumbers when they come round to give you an estimate, before he utters words of wisdom. "Oh, you don't wanna use that," he'll say. "You wanna use what I use." Then he'll tell you how many carp he's caught, the venues he's visited, and how much of a 'following' he has in the carp world. He's very definitely the expert and you ignore his advice at your peril.

"You don't wanna do it like that!" he'll say. "You wanna do it the way I've always done it, like this."

Why isn't he doing it, then? That's what I'd like to know. Why isn't he practising his preaching instead of getting on our nerves, trying to impose his will on others? I'm sure Mr. Enfield must have been inspired to create this character at a water's edge because eventually and predictably, due to the irritation factor, mistakes are made. A cast goes 20 feet up a tree and we get the inevitable, "Now, I don't believe you wanted to do that!"

Valentine's Day massacre

Romance, it has to be said, is not a word one immediately associates with anglers. So, a few years ago, when I had a phone call from the producer of Radio 5's Dirty Tackle, asking me to write and read out on air a three-minute script on the subject, I was a bit taken aback but agreed to the assignment with confidence.

Three minutes? Piece of cake; with my ability to write total drivel on any subject for hours on end, it would be a doddle. An hour later, with computer screen and brain still an absolute blank, I began to think that I'd lost it as complete writer's block set in. Romance was one of the few subjects that had me flummoxed; still, it's only easy to write about what you know, I suppose.

Research in the form of extensive phone calls to fellow fishing widows, revealed that I wasn't alone. There were those who had witnessed many romantic moments at a water's edge but all had been directed at various species of fish, mainly carp. I heard accounts of loving utterances, flowery compliments, the most tender of caresses, promises of eternal devotion...but when I asked if the women had ever been on the receiving end of all this demonstrative affection the general reply was 'not very often, and only when they want something'.

Clearly, something should be done about it. Someone should point out a few things to anglers, and my circle of fishing widows urged me to speak up on their behalf. I have already done my bit for romance over the air-waves but for those of you who didn't hear the early morning, three minute, cough-and- you've-missed-it, broadcast I've reproduced the script for you. I have to tell you that none of the advice I offered came to fruition in my own relationship, or those of my friends, but if just one angler can be saved from his own folly, then my job will have been done.

'Good morning anglers!
Notice anything special about today? Anything on your mind? Do you feel a slight stirring in your heart this morning? All right, your loins, then? No? I thought not.

Today is supposed to be the most romantic day of the year and I bet most of you are checking your maggots for spots, poking your crabs, playing with your worms or tying various small bits of metal to nylon twine, without a passing thought for the woman of your dreams.

It's common knowledge that there's not a lot of romance in anglers' relationships. The average angler's idea of gallantry is to take his wader socks off before getting into bed, and there are those who keep them on, waders and all. It's not because they don't care, they simply don't have the time or the mental space. The small slot in an angler's brain set aside for romance is already half-full with fishy thoughts, so given a couple of passing references to tenderness toward womankind and they have instant overspill. They just can't cope with it.

Passion we get, and plenty of it when adverse weather conditions permit; if it's too foggy, windy or the lake/river's frozen over, a man has to find something else to do, but the art of romance seems to pass most anglers by and that's a bit of a shame. It takes less energy than passion, slightly more time usually, but a little romance can pay huge dividends for very modest effort.

Leaving aside the interference of St Valentine, for a moment, it doesn't take much to keep a fishing widow reasonably happy during the rest of the year. A phone call now and again from a charter boat, a wharf or a water's edge will do it and there's no excuse these days. Even if your mobile phone is out of charge or credit, there's bound to be one angler who will let you use his phone in the interests of domestic harmony. That's all it takes; just a few words to let your loved one know that you haven't dismissed her completely from your memory. Just a text message between casts, for goodness sake! You don't even have to open your mouth for that one.

A friend of mine received one such phone call and was quite impressed by her partner's thoughtfulness. Mind you, it was before the evening pub session. A word of warning here, though, don't phone home post-paralytic; your loved one won't be able to understand a word and will just put the phone down with a weary sigh and dock several brownie points.

My mate's conversation was one-sided and went something like: "I really miss you. It must be all that going up and down on the boat all day." Interspersed by the bunging of 50 pence pieces into a phone box because there was no mobile phone signal in the hotel, there followed a long and detailed account of the capture of a prized 98½lb conger. There was no chance to get a word in edgeways and he didn't ask if she was still horribly pregnant or if his baby had been born while he was at sea and out of range. "See you in a couple of days," he finished up. "Keep everything warm – oh, and I've bought you some presents."

The presents were a 'souvenir from Brixham' tea towel and a mass-produced, small, wooden pirate, purchased at the last minute from one of the many gift shops adjacent to the wharf – and most likely the one next door to the pub. It was a very good quality, attractive tea cloth and the pirate went to live in the bathroom, but her gifts were a far cry from the anticipated lace underwear and French perfume. "At least, he rang." she said, when we were giggling over man's genetic lack of imagination in the gift department. "I didn't get an air-freshener for the car or half-dead flowers from the garage on the way home, this time, and it's the thought that counts."

She was right. It is the thought that matters, you know. An 'I love you' note left in the washing-powder drawer-thingy on the machine so she'll find it when she washes your fishing jeans is a good idea. Pencil the same message on an eggshell or halfway along the toilet roll; rewind it, obviously, you're not a Labrador puppy. Put a note in her make-up bag, the bread bin, there are loads of places if you think about it.

Okay, I understand that you'd have a problem with all that. You couldn't possibly do anything so girlie, you'd feel a complete prat and suppose your mates found out! Have you thought about the future benefits, though? Can you see the potential here? Her reaction, on finding your little offerings, will be 'oh bless!' Possibly 'silly sod, oh bless!' but you'll still get a result. Next time you want to go for a whole weekend including Friday night, carping expedition with the lads, she'll remember. She will offer the obligatory deep sigh and reproachful glance, but you won't get the full scale war because she knows now, doesn't she? You do love her and the urges you have to throw things in, and then retrieve other things out of, water are totally beyond your control and do not detract from your feelings toward her in any way.

So, come on, guys. Do it now! It doesn't have to be Valentine's influence that inspires you. There's bound to be a 24-hour garage nearby, or one of those 'we're open so early until so late that you think we're open all the time,' corner shops. Why not nip out and grab something for your long-suffering loved one. A bar of dark chocolate, which has more romantic impact than Dairy Milk, or a bunch of flowers won't break the bank and, by the way, should be offered before you go fishing. If you present it on your return, it looks like a peace-offering and will dispel any romantic connotations at a stroke.

If you can't be bothered to leave the house, write 'good morning, gorgeous' on a piece of card, attach it to a mug of tea, and deliver to her bedside. Don't go over the top, though, no full breakfasts on trays or she'll think that either you're about to do something she'll disapprove of or that you've done it already and are suffering from guilt.' *Broadcast ends.*

A good percentage of the anglers I know are either divorced already, separated, or living in relationship limbo, hoping things will improve. A little romance, now and again, would go a long way to reduce the suffering. Go on then! Don't just sit there reading!

CHAPTER THREE

MAD AS MARCH AIR

Suffering from wind

It'll be that time of the year again when March winds can play havoc with the lives of normally well-balanced men and women. Walk, or if you're a non-angler and unused to the great outdoors being quite so boisterously outdoor, drive along any stretch of coastline and you'll notice groups of anglers muttering to each other.

They will be congregated on wharves in small groups, while staring dumbly at 30-foot waves crashing over sea walls, or they'll be wandering aimlessly around coastal car parks, sobbing. They may be spotted as they try to cope manfully on windswept beaches with every piece of equipment weighted down around them, their faces contorted by gales and grimaces of concentration as every cast travels one yard forward and several yards back.

They should be given full marks for perseverance but it takes hours before they admit defeat and totter disconsolately away to find a café to sit in while they wait for the wind to drop. The fact that it has been blowing a hooli all night and the forecast is for Hurricane Nobby to hit before lunchtime does not dampen their optimism. In these steamy havens, lone anglers can be observed consuming gallons of strong tea as they watch the raindrops on window panes, or if there's a posse of them, betting on a particular raindrop's progress, until a pub opens and they can drown their sorrows, usually with little effort but sometimes spectacular after-effects.

What baffles me is the fact that they know the conditions are likely to worsen, because they have already every weather prediction transmitted from anywhere. They have tried the Internet, even called the 'ring this number for more information' line in an attempt to find a more favourable forecast. Look out of the window, boys! The conditions are dire and are not likely to improve sufficiently to allow a spot of decent angling; yet they still insist on giving it a go.

Anglers suffer from crippling optimism. 'It will be all right,' they say when you question their motives, and/or mental health. 'The wind's bound to drop this afternoon. It can't blow like this indefinitely.' Maybe not, but you and I know from experience that it's only likely to ease up after they've been at work for an hour on Monday morning.

If it's a Saturday tempest, they'll say, 'Maybe tomorrow!' They seem to expect a sudden calm overnight and are always disappointed when they don't awake to serene, August conditions. My own anglers were in and out of bed all night, peering through the chinks in the curtains like elderly ladies on Neighbourhood Watch duty; as if their vigil was going to make the slightest difference to nature's way.

We lived on the coast and would quite often hear of our local lifeboat being called out to rescue anglers in small craft that had broken anchor in high winds, and were being dragged rapidly toward the Bermuda Triangle. I've heard the Chief Angler condemn the irresponsibility of 'idiots who go out on the water in this weather', but I knew he would go given half a chance, that's if his skipper hadn't had more sense and a considerable amount of respect for his boat.

Just whistle!

Speaking of boats, I sometimes receive phone calls from number one son in distant locations. One memorable conversation was from the boat he was aboard, at anchor 'just off the Needles'. He was working on a feature for a fishing magazine and knows I worry about him when he's working away. He rang me to offer reassurance that, at 30-odd years old, he really is grown up enough to look after himself.

I asked him the usual maternal questions. Had he got his asthma medication? Was he wearing clean underwear? Was he warm enough? What had he eaten in the previous 24 hours?

"For goodness sake, Ma," he muttered impatiently as I went through an intensive interrogation on his well-being. "There's a massive swell. The boat's all over the place and I can hardly stand up, let alone worry about all that malarkey. I'm all right, though. I'm wearing an amazing, state of the art, flotation suit and I've caught a couple of cod."

"Oh, good for you," I said. "I suppose that makes it all right, then."

Never mind the fact that he is adrift in an open boat in extreme weather and without his mother or his wife for protection. He has caught two cod, so all the discomfort and possible dangers must be disregarded. I should have known that, but what was he playing at? He was supposed to be putting my mind at rest not leaving me worried sick in case he fell over the side into sub-zero, raging torrents of salty liquid, his only protection a wearable life-raft thingy with a whistle on it. What's the whistle for, anyway? Who's going to hear it in a force eight gale? It's not only anglers who suffer from wind; we fishing widows/mums have our fair share of agony, too.

Spectator sport

Freshwater anglers don't suffer quite so much. They don't have restraining orders put upon them in the form of being unable to get out on a boat. There is a certain amount of anguish involved, though. Casting is made more difficult and quite a bit of tackle can be lost, even by experts, let alone inexperienced anglers who have not yet learned to judge wind speed and direction. If no allowance is made for a line, blown off course, they end up climbing trees in order to unhook tackle surrounded by bundles of leaves and twigs. I know of one angler who lost a favourite brolly when it took off in a particularly violent squall and kebab-ed itself too far up the side of a tree to enable retrieval.

Observing the behaviour of anglers in windy conditions can be quite entertaining, especially if you're ensconced inside a well-pegged-down bivvy. In fact, March can be one long cabaret. The spectator sport begins before you even leave the house if your anglers are running about in the garden, chasing maggot tubs under shrubs and round the back of trees until they are able to trap them in a corner. Camo jackets, oilskins or romper suits, left pegged to a washing line overnight 'for an airing', must be retrieved from next-door's pergola where they have blown during a particularly furious force eight during the hours of darkness. Being nominated to knock next-door to ask if I could have their clothes back, was always a small price to pay for the entertainment provided.

Lakeside bivvies, if not anchored with sturdy bivvy pegs, can blow about sufficiently to dislodge the angler from his bed chair. This can cause untold distress and inconvenience; not just to the afflicted, but also to other anglers in the vicinity as the victim goes into Sarah Bernhardt mode and queens it up dramatically on the bank. There's no guarantee of a comforting cuppa for the poor soul, either.

Apart from the fact that it is nigh on impossible to light a Coleman stove without a considerable amount of paying attention and strategic placement, his mates will be giggling too much to concentrate.

Bivvies must be pitched so that the wind blows directly into the anglers' faces. Natural food is blown to that end of the lake, so it is of the utmost importance that lines are cast into that small area, never mind the discomfort. I have witnessed an angler inside his open bivvy, clutching on to it with both hands, for dear life, to prevent it from taking off. He was prepared to take the risk of hang-gliding across the Channel rather than move to a more sheltered spot with a reduced chance of catching a carp.

Bluster

"You're not going fishing in this, are you, Derek?" asked my mother as she watched her then son-in-law struggle into wellington boots and a waterproof romper suit.

Outside, it was raining a variety of domestic pets. She had just arrived for morning coffee before our weekly and, for me at least, reluctant visit to the supermarket. Mum was soaking wet, brolly in tatters, and looked on in amazement as the Chief Angler grappled with landing-net pole, match rod, medium-sized canvas holdall, and a bucket containing maggots and bread.

"Erm... I just fancied a stroll round the lake," he

waffled. "So I thought I'd take a bit of light tackle...might try a couple of casts...might not...I haven't even taken sandwiches or anything..."

He meant, 'Yes!' Why couldn't he say so? There would have been no arguments, and we wouldn't have tried to dissuade him. We knew he couldn't control a compulsion to be near water; mind you, he only had to step into the garden to be in the middle of a monsoon. Apparently, he felt that he had to try to justify his weird behaviour and there was an uncomfortable silence for several seconds as my mother tried to think of something to say that wasn't, 'are you completely mad?'

We knew he was lying when he'd told us that this visit to the lake was just a whim, because a mate picked him up and had a hamper of food in his car along with a mountain of tackle, so we could tell that it wasn't exactly a spur of the moment idea. After they'd gone, we tried to analyse his behaviour and concluded that it stemmed from the way anglers have to think on their feet when rivals try to discover the baits or rigs they are using. Evasive answers seem to become second nature after a time.

Mea culpa

Are you the mother of embryonic anglers? Who do you blame if the fishing bug seems to bite your kids too fiercely as they try to put fishing before everything else, including their schoolwork? Let me guess.

"It's all your fault," I used to say to the Chief Angler, when our boys were preparing for a fishing trip and the eldest hadn't yet completed his homework. "If you hadn't been so besotted with fishing they wouldn't be doing this. They'd have been quite happy to do schoolwork and get their projects done on time." None of that was true, and we all knew it, but it made me feel better to say it anyway, even though it made not the slightest bit of difference; fishing always came before homework, and looking back, I can see that they were right.

From this...

Do you feel left out when they would rather go and get soaking wet, cold, and thoroughly uncomfortable near water than sit at home with you playing Monopoly or making scale models of the Mary Rose out of toilet roll holders and sticky-backed plastic? Do you get the arse when they sit for hours at a stretch, rearranging tackle boxes, discussing tactics, methods, venues, and speculating on which species could be swimming in the next water they intend to visit, just as soon as they can persuade you to drive them there?

Think twice before you put the boot in, before you blame 'he who has shares in the tackle shop'. There is a strong possibility that your child's obsession with water, which quite often starts in a small way and gradually increases in intensity to include every lake, river, and stretch of coastline, could be down to you after all. Yes, really.

Recently I was forced to review my photo drawer(s). For some time, I had been finding it more and more difficult to force any more prints into the limited space available. Eventually, as I pushed at the front, I heard the inevitable rat-a-tat-tat as old photo wallets overflowed from the back of the drawer and on to the floor space within the drawer unit.

Goodness knows how long this had been going on because when I removed the drawers to have a look, I found photos that hadn't seen the light of day for a scarily long time. Sitting there on the floor, surrounded and completely sidetracked by memorabilia, I found evidence to support the fact that the water fascination from which both of my sons suffer, was more than likely my fault after all. I say 'suffer' but there's no sign of distress unless their desire to be near it is thwarted. Even if the condition

...mine's a pint!...

...she told me there was a fishy in here...

...to this.

is not down to me entirely, it might have been instigated and was certainly encouraged.

Large containers of water in the garden on hot, lazy, summer afternoons, that contained toys to fish out and throw in again might have had some massive impact on infant psyches, for all I know. Maybe the introduction of fishing rods a few years later wasn't the trigger for a lifetime obsession with liquid, after all. Perhaps the initial interest was created by the excitement and joy of finding plastic fish, ducks, and boats at the bottom of an al fresco washing-up bowl.

Still, it could have been worse, couldn't it? If I'd presented them with a climbing frame, they could both be half-way up Everest by now.

NOW you're talkin'.

Pink

I seem to be wearing an awful lot of pink. I hate pink. It makes me think of open-heart surgery or the steak tartare that I ordered once, embarrassingly and many years ago, in a high-class restaurant by mistake, because I wanted to appear sophisticated but didn't realise it was raw meat. It says a fair bit about my personality that I managed to consume best part of it without gagging. It takes a while for me to make a decision about anything, but once I make my mind up to do something, I get on with it.

I shouldn't wear pink, anyway. I've always felt more comfortable in an anonymous monochrome colour combo, with an occasional flash of green or blue when things really need to be livened up a bit, because I've never been a very feminine 'girly' kind of person and pink only seems to amplify my lack of girliness. Sometimes, though, it seems to be the only way to keep warm.

I'll tell you the reason for all this pinkness. The knitting season is upon us and I have a talent for designing and producing original Aran sweaters. It's not as clever as it sounds and I'm not the only one who has a repertoire of Aran stitches and incorporates them into a plain sweater. The results are pretty good though, and because I haven't told anyone how easy it is, my friends are impressed.

I've been trying to knit a new jumper for the winter and so far I've completed five. Trouble is, this season's colours are of the 'spice and/or nature' variety - i.e. browns, terracotta, greens and cream. Every time I sewed one together, a visiting friend or member of my family said something like 'That's really nice. It's freezing up at the lake. I'd love a jumper like that to keep me warm. You *are* clever. What a brilliant pattern. How on earth do you do that? I wish I was artistic, witty, clever like you...' and much more associated but successfully flattering bullshit. They even purloined the matching woolly hats that I manufactured from leftovers.

My immediate family and I are all roughly the same size so I'm wearing pink this winter because it's the only colour that the men in my life refuse to put on their backs.

Fiddling with your tackle

Even though the close season is no longer observed, I remember how it used to be in our household. There was a gradual slowing down toward the end of the freshwater period, and an almost immediate defection to salt water after March 16th every year. It doesn't happen today, because the lakes are open all year round, but I mourn the passing of yet another tradition. There seems to be less and less of it about, these days. I admit to having been dragged, kicking and screaming, into the 21st century; born too late, that's me, but there seems to be no respect for anything anymore. Our lives are being altered, albeit in small chunks at a time so we hardly notice, in the name of modern living and keeping ahead of the times.

There are football teams that seem to be made up of millionaires and/or non-British players, all married to top models or so-called celebrities and their status seems to be as important to them as their sport. My late father, who played for Leyton Orient before the war, got 12/6d a game (that's about 62p) and nothing at all if the match was cancelled. He told me that there was no such thing as football hooliganism then. In those days, good manners were taught, both in schools and at home, and people learned how to be a good loser; no one even thought about punching the living daylights out of an opposing fan. Mind you, they didn't go in for booze at football matches then either, they'd have a pint or two in the local once safely back at home; maybe that's a contributory factor to today's violence, along with an 'it's all about me' attitude.

My old dad would turn in his urn if he could see how commercial his beloved football has become. It's all about money, these days, or so it seems, and sadly, that applies to so many facets of our society.

Even cricket, our most traditional game and so far not quite as commercially obscene as soccer, but don't hold your breath, has been forced into becoming trendy. I thought there was an American baseball match in progress when tuned in to Sky, one evening last summer. There they were, our boys in what should have been classical white - except they were in green, complete with sponsors' logos, and getting severely stuffed, as usual, by their opponents dressed in similar outfits of commercialised dove grey.

All that has little to do with the close season, I know, but that's what I'm leading up to. This three-month period of respite for the fish and their habitat was introduced in 1923 to protect them when spawning, and to allow the environment to recover from constant angling traffic. The strategy was successful for 70-odd years, until the law was revoked in 1996 and a byelaw modification meant that there was no longer a statutory demand for closure. Providing the venue was not registered as being of scientific interest, managers of all stillwaters, plus canals, had the option of closing or not. Most of them opted to open and, to me, it begs the question of financial gain over the welfare of the fish, particularly after commercial interests last year were putting pressure on the Environment Agency to withdraw the close season on rivers, too - or maybe that's just me being cynical.

In my opinion, our lakes and rivers should be given the chance to recover from nine months of regular traffic. I've heard quite a few anglers say that they regret the 'do as you like' licence given to lake owners from March through June, when traditionally, the lakes were closed. Most of them still take advantage of the freedom, mind you, but that's only because of the way anglers' minds work. Knowing that there is no restriction, they have no choice in the matter. They don't go because they want to; they just have to, and mostly under protest, or so they say. If there were a law stating that they couldn't go, then it would be out of their hands and an entirely different matter.

The first season after the new rule came into force, one of our local club waters came up with an answer to the close season dilemma of 'should we open, or not?' There are three lakes on this particular complex and the management team decreed that each of them would open for a month; one from March to April, another from April to May and the third, from May until the glorious 16th June. This system would allow the two closed lakes a two-month chance of recovery. The third lake is the Blue Lagoon, and the most popular water in the complex, so the old excitement returned, in a way. Even though it was only closed for about six weeks, there was still a certain amount of anticipation and that buzz of casting a line at the last stroke of midnight on the 16th.

We thought it was a great idea and everybody in the club was happy. Some of the anglers I knew on other venues that didn't have a similar system said that the build up of excitement, which used to mount in the few weeks before the start of the season, had been lost forever and they missed it dreadfully. I can't see it, myself. There seems to be a fair amount of excitement before every single fishing trip in most angling households, and there could always be a self-imposed, three-month lay-off if it's excitement they want. No self-control, some anglers.

So it's that time of the year again, for the coarse angling side of things. It's a well-known fact that those who fish the briny are somehow able to find the time to fiddle with their tackle all year round, but coarse fishermen have only a selected couple of months during which their bits and pieces can be seriously played about with.

My house was taken over by testosterone-fuelled activity, and woe betide any female who got caught in the crossfire. Since I was the only woman within spitting distance, I made a habit of going out to a coffee shop with other fishing widows who were undergoing the same siege-like conditions. We compared notes and realised that we were all in the same boat, to coin a phrase.

In every room, there are items of fishing equipment getting an 'airing,' being oiled, scrubbed or generally overhauled in readiness for the re-opening of their favourite lake. Lounge carpets have disappeared under a sea of floats, rigs, exploded - but soon to be re-assembled - reels, and a variety of rods wait expectantly in gardens, to be washed down gently with cotton wool and Johnson's baby shampoo before being re-polished.

Our kitchen sinks are full to the brim with bait containers and tackle boxes, soaking away last season's detritus; baths had things floating in them, because they have to test their rigs and home-made pop-ups in there; where else? The general ambience of our usually fairly organised households had become one of complete chaos.

Not content with spreading themselves and their toys over every flat surface, my anglers also commandeered the TV. They had to watch something, they said, predominantly, Sky fishing programmes, or well-worn fishing videos, while they were in overhaul mode. For this reason everything took three times as long as it would have, had a Screaming Reel or John Wilson not sidetracked them. I knew from experience that to attempt any kind of conversation would be futile unless the adverts were on. My only recourse was to visit the nearest chocolate shop, drive to a friend's house, whose husband is

It's all got to be sorted.

heavily into golf, but washes his…erm…equipment at the club house, and stay there for a few hours until I considered it safe to return home.

It's a wise move to leave the house, anyway, especially when they take over the cooker, too. While one of them is dreaming of Rex Hunt, the others manufacture boilies at a rate of knots, filling any available breathable air space with concentrated fumes of Monster Crab, or Squid and Scopex, laced with strawberry or tropical fruit. That's not exactly conducive to quality chocolate consumption, I'm telling you. I'm a traditionalist, and to enjoy chocolate, I need to be able to breathe. Apart from the plaintive cry, which hung in the air as I made a dash for it, that fishing makes you hungry, even when transmitted by the moving wireless, they didn't miss me.

Toys all over the place.

Maybe I'm in a minority, but it seems to me that there are too many people, in minor officialdom, changing too much of our lives, just for the sake of it and despite all the inconvenience of having spring weekends disrupted, I still think the close season should be enforced. I can't help it; as I said, I'm a traditionalist.

CHAPTER FOUR

APRIL SHOWERS

Close season blues

It was always a bit of a disappointment when my family's favourite lake was closed for a couple of months. They didn't enjoy fishing the other two lakes in the complex quite as much; the best carp, they said, were in the Blue Lagoon, but my anglers are hard, they are men. One of them even has tattoos. They could do without the Blue, temporarily. They could even go without fishing altogether, if they wanted to, if they really tried, for two months until it re-opened. In fact, they thought they would. Carping would not even cross their minds. They do have a life outside fishing, you know. Oh, yeah? Is that right? Do they think I'm somebody else when they're spouting all that nonsense?

It lasted about a fortnight before it all became too much to bear. By the third weekend, they told me that it was only just over a month until the lake re-opened and that there were vital preparation jobs to be done.

They had already spent best part of three months tarting up their tackle. Now, it appears, it has to be done all over again. So, the garden was taken over by bivvies, opened up either to search for potential leaks or to prevent mildew from forming, depending on the weather conditions at the time. Newly scrubbed sleeping bags were set to dry on the washing line. Nets, carp mats, tackle bags, and anything remotely washable in a front loader, all were spread to dry on grass which needed cutting but could not be mown until all the assorted paraphernalia had been removed from our own personal bit of grass, and transferred to the communal bits at the lake.

Reels and lakeside cookers were taken apart, cleaned, lubricated, and reassembled at the dining room table. A vice was attached to one of the antique, solid oak sides so that a treasured rod could be held steady within a

And just where am I supposed to hang the washing?

brand new tea-towel, while a new ring was whipped on to the tip, then varnished and left overnight. This could not possibly be disturbed until it was dry so the family had to eat off trays on laps, something I used to hate.

The kitchen resembled a bombsite. Boilie making was in full spate and there was a sink full of breakfast pots waiting to be washed up because I hadn't had a chance to get at them, and the boilie maker couldn't possibly have done it before he started. He had a far more important job to do and could not spare the time for such demeaning tasks. Dishes festered while boilies took priority and I was not allowed anywhere near the kitchen. Not that I particularly wanted to go; besides the stench of Monster Crab and Blueberry combo being almost unbearable, I might have been asked to 'keep an eye on that stock pot while I make a phone call'.

Okay, I give up.

Translated, this means 'boil 25 boilies at a time (there are hundreds waiting) for two minutes while I go and chat to my mates for an hour.' Could I prepare dinner for tonight, while I waited? No, that would not be possible. I would lose concentration and, God forbid, I might spoil a batch or two. We'll grab a take-away but I could, if I fancied a walk, go out to buy another two-dozen eggs. 'But come straight back, only go to the egg shop. I'll need those eggs in about half an hour.'

This ritual was performed every weekend for the remaining five weeks until the lake re-opened, interspersed with pleasant, angler-free hours at a time, when they rushed off to make sure that the Blue Lagoon was recovering nicely, or to reconnoitre another water which they had no intention of fishing anyway.

Came the day when they could return to their chosen venue and it was all worthwhile. The freezer was crammed to bursting with every recommended flavour of boilie, plus some new ones which happened by accident because the boilie-maker had been standing too close to my spice cupboard to avoid temptation. All the carping equipment had been refurbished or replaced and they were off for at least a full 12 hours at a stretch. You don't have to show me heaven. I know exactly what it will be like.

Hubble, bubble, toil and trouble – or ten easy steps to making your own boilies.

1. Clear the sink, or get your wife/partner/mother to do it for you since it is women's work, washing up.

Getting ready to roll; note the full sink.

The Chief Angler once recoiled in horror because there was a fork left in ours. "Can't do anything until the sink's cleared, sort it out," he said, and walked away from it. Seems that if you have a willy, you can't pick up cutlery.

2. Wash hands scrupulously clean in sink, now minus fork and full of hot, soapy water. Nothing can be allowed to contaminate a boilie mix. Strange how he never washed his hands before eating, making sandwiches, or anything else come to think of it.

3. Half fill a very expensive, top of the range, only used at Christmas for puddings, 6-pint cooking pot with water and place on hob to boil while you read the eggs. That means study the little dates printed on each egg in an attempt to get hold of the very freshest ones; the

family can consume the others, they're not as discerning as carp.

4. Pour several tablespoonfuls of boilie mix into a brand new Ikea mixing bowl, then add two eggs. Complain gently, at this point, that the eggs do not 'bounce' as really fresh eggs should.

5. Hands in. Stir it around a bit then add a little more mix so that the whole glutinous mess forms into some kind of dough. If it's too wet, add a little more of the base mix.

6. Wash hands before touching the bag of base mix and do not bother to dry them. This will allow the bag to slip slightly, thereby accidentally adding a little too much mix; then exclaim 'Oh Shit!' before adding another egg.

7. Wash mix off hands. By this stage in the game, there will be more mix in the sink than in the mixing bowl, but the final product should be just damp enough to roll between finger and thumb.

8. Ask your wife/partner/mother, 'Is that too wet, do you think?' (poke, feel, roll), as if I can tell just by looking at it; I was not allowed to touch. When convinced that the texture is perfect, roll into small, but perfectly formed, balls, using shop bought boilies as a guideline for size. I have to say at this point that number one son witnessed this entire trauma and by the time it was his turn to be bitten by the 'make your own boilies' bug, he'd invested in a rolling table and associated

equipment. Not at all stupid, our Dave.

9. Place a dozen boilies on a wide, slotted spoon and lower gently into the now rapidly boiling water, holding the spoon just below the surface. Be vigilant. The movement of the boiling water will cause the boilies to dance on the spoon and the effect can be like one of those computer games that require hand to eye coordination. The

Not stupid, the eldest, he's gone technical.

spoon must be constantly jiggled in order to retain the cooking boilies in their rightful place, ensuring that a boilie is not lost into the bowels of the pan, but only for about 40 seconds.

10. Continue in this insane manner until all the boilies are boiled. The finished items should be placed on spread-out newspaper on every available square inch of downstairs floor space, and then allowed to dry off and become cool before being placed in small plastic bags and frozen.

A couple of tips, here; when you get fed up with rolling boilies to scale, you can, apparently, change tactics and create little baby ones as freebies to throw round your

Half-time. A man's gotta wee, but leave the lid on to stop it all going off the boil.

hook bait; and you can mix flavourings into the basic mix or dip them in something unspeakable before you freeze them.

Finally, leave the kitchen in a terrible mess and then tell the wife/partner/mother not to worry because you have already cleaned it all up. She will tell you to leave the clearing up to her in future, since she has to do it all again anyway after your pathetic attempts at housework - and, incidentally, we know that's why you do it!

The satisfaction of boasting to your mates, after you've caught a carp that clearly does not have a discerning palate, that you actually made a successful bait all by yourself is, I'm told, a 'man' thing and boosts a flagging ego no end.

Thermal raspberries

Those thermal romper suits are no good for keeping people warm, you know, well, certain people. All right, me then. There I was, warming up the car engine one unseasonably cold and frosty Saturday morning while Himself loaded all and absolutely sundry into every crevice of the back seat and boot. He eventually dived, fully rompered-up, into the passenger seat, sweating like a pig, and began to play with all the electric window buttons.

I was dressed in normal car driving gear for the time of year, pair of jeans, sweater and light jacket and I'd got a vulnerable neck which was only just getting used to being exposed to the elements after half a century of being covered by long hair. The last thing my emergent neck needed was a blast of easterly breeze, but that's what it got, all the way to the lake. "I'm so hot," he said, encased in all-weather green. "Gotta have all the windows open or I'll have a stroke. Can't you go any faster?"

Getting a stiff neck and seriously chilled was the lesser of two evils, though. I'd tried insisting that he travelled to the lake in jeans and jumper, and then donned the suit on arrival at the venue, which he agreed was a good idea, in theory. In practice, though the outfit had to be climbed into while the boot lid was open, and very definitely before anything could be unpacked. Don't ask me, I've no idea why, but I had to wait for a good ten minutes in a considerable draught while he struggled with the zips and Velcro, which makes rude noises, incidentally.

He told me that every time he tried to extricate anything from one of the many pockets by pulling on the Velcro, it sounded as if he had broken wind and the only way he could retain his dignity was to stare disapprovingly at the angler in an adjacent swim.

I came to the conclusion that thermal romper suits are more trouble than they're worth; besides the suffering caused to innocent fishing widows, they encourage anti-social behaviour and should be taken off the market immediately.

Carp versus cod

It's not a wise move to try to introduce dedicated sea anglers to carp fishing, we found out, particularly if the weather conditions are not perfect. Here in the south-east, we'd had little rain for a couple of months until the 12 hours that the Chief Angler chose to spend at our local club water in the company of a couple of sea-angling friends. It began to rain ten minutes after they arrived and didn't stop until the following afternoon.

They had just the one brolly between them that had been taken along 'just in case', fortunately. This was commandeered by the two aliens, who sat huddled beneath it for the duration, like Tweedledum and Tweedledee. Tweedledum developed a habit of looking at his watch every ten minutes or so, and calculating aloud how much longer he had to wait until the pubs opened, while the Chief Angler prepared rods, baited up and cast out in the pouring rain, clad only in T-shirt and rapidly-shrinking jeans.

He had a good day. He caught several fair-sized roach, a three-pound bream and a couple of tench as part of his cabaret act trying to keep his colleagues entertained while showing them that it was possible to enjoy 'being there', regardless of weather conditions, and the fact that the carp rods were showing no sign of life. Eventually, he gave in, if only to put a stop to the querulous remarks about the trip being a complete waste of time and how his mates could murder a pint. He agreed to pack everything up and go to the pub.

"Been on a fishing trip?" asked the landlord, stating the bleedin' obvious, since they were all soaking wet, covered in mud and had all ordered large brandies. They always ventured into his establishment in a similar condition after every sea-fishing trip and he had jumped to a conclusion. "Any cod out there?" he asked, innocently.

"Bin carp fishing," muttered Tweedledum. "Bloody waste of time, that was. Can't understand what they see in it. Didn't see hide or hair of a carp. Never again!"

The Chief Angler kept his own counsel and didn't mention that they'd had no hope of seeing hide or hair of anything, since they had been stuck under a brolly without moving for four hours. He bought them both a pint and agreed to differ.

April fool

The youngest thrust a scroll of paper under my nose on April 1st. "I've had a terrible day," he said, grinning, "and it's all your fault."

He hadn't told anyone, at the engineering firm where he worked, what I do for a living. Either the subject was never broached or he was too embarrassed to admit to the fact that his picture had been published in a national magazine. That's how you get even, you know, be an embarrassment to your children.

Simon had reckoned without the 'carp anglers are everywhere' syndrome, though, and when he walked into the workshop on this particular morning, there on the wall was the following message in the form of a large poster.

The photo of Simon clutching a small common to his bosom, and previously published in Carpworld magazine, had been hugely reproduced underneath and they took the mickey out of him all day. What a result!

WANTED
for fish molestation
and other nefarious practices
REWARD $10,000

Beavering up

Speaking of practical jokes, I used to be on the receiving end quite often. I was far too trusting, at the time, and very definitely gullible. On board ship on our way to Australia in the 60s, our table steward asked me to take my napkin down to my cabin, wash and iron it and bring it back in time for breakfast the following morning. We were about to cross the Equator, he explained. The water goes down the plughole in the opposite direction, on the other side, and this would bugger up the ship's laundry. I did it, without question. 'Thick' would have been a good word to describe me, then. I improved with age.

Anyway, back to the plot. Royal Mail had tried to deliver a parcel to me while I was out, but I knew what it was and who'd sent it. A mate had bought me a 'lucky' plastic otter, which I had been instructed to take with me every time I went fishing. Aah, bless! How thoughtful. What a lovely bloke. I've met some fantastic people while working within the angling scene.

There was a problem, though. The card shoved through the door by the frustrated postie told me that the parcel had been addressed to Rosie Beaver and I now had to go to the sorting office and retrieve the package. I set off, anticipating trouble.

"I've come to pick up a parcel," I said, as I handed over the card on arrival at the depot.
"Righty ho," said the calm and unflustered guy behind the counter. "Have you got some ID?"
"Erm…yes…" I just knew this was going to happen, "…but the name on my driving licence doesn't tally precisely with the name on the parcel."
Did he want to know why? Oh, yes!

"I quite often camp out with a load of blokes," I said, by way of explanation, "and for my birthday, last year,

Lucky for some.

a friend gave me a soft, fluffy beaver which I have to secure to the top of my tent. All beavers...erm...bivvies look the same in the dark so, this way, they all know where the female element lives and they don't come charging in. The sender addressed it to Rosie Beaver as a joke. The parcel doesn't contain a beaver, though, it's an otter."

By this time, the poor man had stepped back several paces, worked up a sweat and was becoming more and more nervous.

"I see," he said, clearly not understanding at all. "Technically..." he had a stab at rational thought. "Technically, we shouldn't allow you to have the parcel but..."

I could read his mind. 'I'll just give it to you so you'll go away', that's what he was thinking.

"He couldn't find a plastic beaver in the shop, you see," I gabbled on. "So he bought me an otter instead." I felt quite sorry for the bloke as he scuttled off. He was back in double-quick time, thrust the parcel at me, and slammed shut the glass door of his cubbyhole.

So, thanks a lot, Elton. All the postal workers in our area are now only too well aware of my beaver/otter situation and, as my neighbour's husband works for the GPO, in the same sorting office, so is everyone else on nodding acquaintance in the neighbourhood. Cosmic!

Stick it on a hook

They will use anything for bait if they think it might give them an edge: Maltesers, bread pudding, bread dipped in pilchard juice, insects, aromatherapy oils, the baby's rose hip syrup...you name it and they've probably tried it. Inside every angler, there's a budding research and development chemist trying to get out.

I've always loved to cook. It's one of the few things that I'm good at and I could relate strongly to the experimental flavouring sessions performed by my anglers during boilie making, because I did it, too. The only difference is that my culinary trials were not usually chucked into a lake; the family were obliged to eat them to keep me happy.

Boiled gammon, spiced with black peppercorns, mustard seed, bay leaves, and garlic had seemed like a good idea, accompanied by creamed spuds, homemade pease pudding, and butter beans in a redcurrant/port sauce. Butter beans are always disguised with some kind of sauce because I know the family are not keen. Redcurrants would counteract the fat in the bacon and besides I was out of parsley. They were very tasty too, for those of you who are thinking, 'Yik!'

"I'll only have a few of those," said number one son, peering over my shoulder as I dished up. "What's that red stuff on 'em?"
I'd made loads, as I always did, forever over-estimating their appetites or forgetting that for a while, the youngest survived on sausage sandwiches, burgers, chips and cornflakes.

"Don't throw them away!" exclaimed the fruit of my loins, as I made for the waste bin with superfluous beans; I rarely waste anything but soup made with leftover butter beans and redcurrants didn't appeal, no matter how much port was in the original concoction. "They look okay. Save them for me."

I thought I'd got a result. At last, I'd created gourmet butter beans that they approved of, after decades of trying to persuade them to experiment with food and to eat vegetables other than peas and carrots. I felt quite emotional.

"Save them until the week-end,' he said. 'I'll stick 'em on a hook."

Cats

Very rarely did I put my foot down and demand that I see some of my friends after dark. It was okay if the anticipated evening visitors were anglers, because then the Chief Angler would have something to talk about over the port, but some of my female friends and their partners had no interest in fishing and so were banished to the hours of daylight and 'coffee mornings'. Against my better judgement, I decided that the time had come to assert myself, and I invited a few friends and their partners for dinner on a Saturday night. What could possibly go wrong? The Chief Angler might even get to like non-angling people, you could never tell.

My guests were seated at the dining table with cutlery at the ready by the time Himself, who had been carping all day, arrived home all hot and bothered. He dumped nets and carp sack outside the back door, hurriedly put the rest of the gear away, grabbed a shower, a change of clothes, opened a bottle of wine and joined our guests, with seconds to spare before I served the first course. I counted myself lucky if he arrived home in time for the first course (for first course read 'at all'), so I didn't take too much notice of his movements and besides, I was up to my armpits in lasagne and scallopini; the wine was Italian and I'd worked my menu around that.

Everything was going surprisingly smoothly, mainly due to the fact that the Chief Angler had managed, as usual, to steer the conversation around to his favourite subject. My friends were humouring him and trying to appear interested for my sake, and they were making a pretty convincing job of it, too. By the time we'd consumed the antipasti, one of the men was booked in for a sea-fishing trip on the following Sunday, and I'd made arrangements for a coffee morning with his wife for a counselling session in the ways of fishing widowhood. I knew it wasn't going to stop at just the one trip.

The Chief Angler seemed to be enjoying himself. He was halfway through a second bottle of Valpolicella, and had just reached the stage of showing off his tackle, when there was a loud and determined knock at the front door. A stony-faced young woman stood there and begged admittance to our back garden where, she said, she could hear her cat miaowing in distress. We hadn't heard a thing over the chink of glasses, fishing related anecdotes and Lionel Richie as background music, but because she insisted, we invited her in, opened the back door and there was her brain-dead feline with its claws caught up in one of the dumped landing nets.

"Oh, baby!" our alien visitor cooed. "Have these nasty people hurt you, then?"
"Excuse me! I've been feeding the five thousand, and no one's touched your idiot cat." I defended myself against animal cruelty. "How was I to know that your stupid animal had trespassed into my garden and tangled itself up?"

She lost her temper, accused me of deliberately ignoring her cat's cries for assistance, ranted and raved about fish feeling pain, people who eat meat and the irresponsibility of folk who go fishing and leave potentially hazardous equipment all over the place. She threatened to sue and marched off indignantly clasping her precious and, I swear, smug pet to her bosom.

Thereafter, we made sure that the nets were hung on a washing line so that only birds, bats and flying insects could become entangled. They never did. Clearly, they have more sense than nurtured cats with unclipped talons. So, there you have it; another cautionary tale. There seem to be so many hurdles to overcome in this fishing lark.

CHAPTER FIVE

DARLING BUDS OF MAY

Led by the nose

May heralds the preparation for conger fishing in June. This can involve several time-consuming exercises, one of which is the manufacture of lead weights. This can be a difficult time of year for anglers if they are freshwater fishermen, too. While they are preparing for conger, they can't be out keeping an eye on carp, tench, or barbel, and vice versa; either way, you will have frustrated anglers to deal with. Before the abolition of the close season, conger time used to coincide with the start of the freshwater offensive in the middle of June, so it was important to get the preparation for both conger and their freshwater cousins over with as soon as possible.

A number of large lumps of lead piping were kept handy, sometimes for years at a time, in our garden shed and retrieved when deemed necessary, to be melted down. You should take careful note of the warning signs in this tale because there will almost certainly be a graphic 'how to' article in one of the angling publications at this time of year. This will inspire your anglers into having a go and you may find yourself in a similar situation, although to be fair, the published weight-making instructions usually suggest that the manufacture is carried out sensibly in a workshop or barbecue area and not in a domestic kitchen.

I used to teach small children the art of piano playing, between looking after the family, cooking, cleaning, washing, ironing...all the usual chores, and many other activities which are traditionally carried out by the male of the species. That is, of course, unless they're dedicated anglers, when digging the garden, decorating, cleaning the car, the unbunging of drains, gutters and toilets becomes women's work. Fortunately, most of my pupils were the offspring of friends so the unusual behaviour of my menfolk was looked upon with an open mind, and accepted as part of the fun of venturing across our threshold.

How anyone ever learned anything musical during these half-hour stints defies belief. More often than not, they were constantly interrupted by 'Where's...?' 'What have you done with...?' 'Could you just hold this, while I...?', but the youngsters enjoyed the lessons so much, probably because of the novelty value, that they achieved good results.

One very warm Saturday morning in May, I was offering instruction to the daughter of a good friend. Fortunately, as it turned out, her parents possess a similar sense of humour to mine; otherwise, I could have found myself on the receiving end of a lawsuit. The piano lesson was progressing nicely. Hannah was a very bright little girl musically, and she had practised her pieces until her little fingers ached. After ten minutes, though, she made repeated and, for her, uncharacteristic mistakes. I couldn't work it out.

"Are you tired, sweetheart?" I asked her. "Did you stay up late last night? Do you feel poorly?"

She started to cry. "My head feels funny," she said.

Only then did I realise that in the kitchen, one room away and with connecting doors wide open, the Chief Angler and his mate were in the throes of melting down lead-piping in their own small, cast-iron cauldron. They had bought this between them, specifically for the purpose, because they had been told off severely last time after using my best milk saucepan. Unnoticed, fumes had been slowly infiltrating the music room and were very clearly having an adverse effect on Hannah's infant brain.

We opened all the windows, took a musical storybook out into the garden, and sat on the grass, drinking restorative lemonade for the last ten minutes of the lesson. When Hannah's father came to collect her, it was with some trepidation that I explained why his daughter was feeling a bit wobbly. As I said, his sense of humour is a good one, so it was okay but it could have been considerably dodgy had Hannah been the health and safety inspector's daughter.

I castigated my anglers for their lack of forethought and patience. Hannah was the last lesson of the morning, for goodness sake. Couldn't they have waited 30 minutes until she had gone home? They thought I was making a huge fuss about nothing, shrugged, and said 'there was no harm done'. I heard them discussing PMT in hushed tones, so I went for a walk in case I killed someone. By the time I returned, the mate had gone home to his own nice, clean kitchen, I'd calmed down, put it all down to experience, and vowed to think no more about it – until next summer, when I would take precautions.

Some hours later, when it was time to cook supper, I began to have symptoms of what I thought was a migraine, hardly surprising after the stress of the day. One of the warning signs of an imminent migraine attack is a mild disorientation and everything in the cooker area looked slightly out of bonk. I took a couple of pills, hoping to stave off the headache side of things until I'd managed to feed the family. If you've never experienced a migraine, let me tell you that once the pain starts, you have no chance of standing upright, let alone cooking anything.

I had decided to concoct a powerful chicken curry, a family favourite that on this occasion was to serve a dual purpose, i.e. to feed a multitude while dispelling any last traces of lead fumes as it cooked. As I began to throw chopped vegetables and garlic into hot oil, the pan listed to the left and slid off the hob, spreading its contents over an unexpectedly wide area of kitchen floor. Definitely a migraine on the way, I thought, clumsiness being another symptom. I cleared up the mess, started again and the same thing happened.

Closer investigation was required, so I stood back and looked at the hob. Apparently, the heat generated by the melting of lead in a red-hot crucible on a domestic cooker, also goes downward on to the square, alloy, saucepan holders, which buckle slightly. They look all right from a distance and you don't notice the damage until you try to balance a pan on them. "Beyond repair," the bloke in the kitchen shop told me when I took one in to show him when purchasing replacements. "What on earth have you been doing?"

The aftermath of weight making can continue for several weeks. Small globules of lead may be discovered lurking in corners, above and below eye-level, where they have been missed during the initial clean up; usually perfunctory if performed by the perpetrators. Goodness only knows how lead fragments got into the cupboards but they did, and the cutlery drawer and the washing machine. The whole kitchen area became a game show site – 'hunt the poisonous substance before it zaps you.'

There were strange splodges and swirls outside in the garden. My anglers used to leave the back door open while in construction mode, so that they could flick risen lead scum deftly from the top of the saucepan and on to the concrete patio area. The resulting intricate, silver patterns made it seems as if our snail population had held a midnight rave; disco snails on Ecstasy, at the very least.

So, the only way to avoid all the hassle of a lead-making session is to go out for the day and not return until all danger of your possible involvement has passed. This includes cleaning up, the storage of cooled off weights, humping full and very heavy boxes of bright, shiny lead weights to the garden shed and much more. Before you leave the house, you should first hide everything that you don't want them to use. I speak from experience. If your best and sharpest secateurs go missing, it'll be because they've been used to cut up the lead. You'll never prune another rose with them and it will be your own fault for not taking precautions.

Irish stew

Because of a number of financial and domestic crises that always seemed to occur in the summertime, holidays were non-events. The family never had holidays. The Chief Angler did. He would go on fishing trips for weeks at a time but 'they are not holidays; it's just fishing', apparently. There came a time, though, when I was determined to get away for at least a week and in anticipation of the event, asked Himself to pop into the Irish Tourist Board offices, situated adjacent to his studio in London, to pick up a couple of brochures so I could get an idea of price and accommodation.

Having carried out his quest successfully, he returned armed with a sizeable bundle of literature. 'Angling Breaks in Ireland.' 'Fishing Holidays on the Shannon.' 'Ireland for the Angler.' 'Fishing Cottages on the Lakes of Ireland.' 'Self-Catering for the Irish Angler.' There were dozens of them.

"Erm.. I don't recall mentioning anything about fishing," I said, foolishly. "I fancied a five-star hotel in Dublin, heritage tours, historical walks and Irish music in Guinness-fumed pubs in the evenings - or a horse-drawn caravan tour." Stereotypical, I know, but that's what I wanted.

You should have seen his face. A number of emotions flashed by; shock, bewilderment, then anguish, closely followed by dogged determination. "You can't go to Ireland without going fishing!" he exclaimed. "What's the matter with you? Use some sense."

I thought about it and changed my mind. I would be the only driver; the Chief Angler didn't drive and the boys were not old enough at the time. There would be three lots of fishing gear to cart around and two teenagers in close proximity to each other, who argued all the time even when they had space. The result would have been an extremely uncomfortable and stressful journey. Once all the fishing stuff was ensconced in my average-sized car there was little room for people; passengers just had to squash in where they could.

Once at our destination, we'd be camping, in effect. "Why pay out a small fortune to travel across the Irish Sea when you can bivvy-up at home?" I argued, as the CA tried to change my mind back again. He'd become quite enthusiastic about the prospect of a fishing holiday, once he'd read the brochures.

Clearly, I didn't understand these things, I was told. There were different fish to be caught abroad, strategy would be a challenge, and all manner of watercraft would have to be deployed in an attempt to catch the fish of Erin. Extensive research would have to be undertaken before any thought of which part of the Emerald Isle we decided to grace with our presence. It would be a full-time job trying to cope with it all. Then there was the dilemma of licences. Were they the same as in the UK? Probably not, it was decided. That would have to be dealt with as a matter of urgency. "You can do that, can't you? And when we've booked it, you'll have to find the phone number of the nearest tackle shop in case we run out of anything..."

I speculated on who would be doing all the shopping, food preparation and cooking, cleaning, making up beds, smoothing out sleeping bags, washing pants, visiting the tackle shop after the first foray because one of them had forgotten a vital ingredient...oh, that'd be me then. I forgot the whole thing and breathed a sigh of relief. It was almost like being on holiday.

Let's have a party!

Another name should be thought up for the work party days. My youngest used to shudder at the sound of that four-letter word ending in K, and had great difficulty getting out of bed on the mornings of these events. Once he got there, of course, he enjoyed every minute; it was just the thought of 'work' on a Sunday. I think they should be called 'Take the mickey out of the older anglers parties,' because that's what most of the youngsters seemed to do most of the time, despite the fact that it was the old'uns with the required stamina to get things done.

Work parties are an essential part of any club's annual curriculum. Without the input of volunteers, essential maintenance would go by the wayside, to the detriment of fish, habitat, and ultimately the anglers themselves. Everyone moans about feeling obliged to contribute but in reality, once they've got stuck in, they seem to enjoy it. I'm sure it's a kind of 'primitive man, building a mud hut' syndrome, making a living space comfortable for himself and his companions, which somehow overrides the male brain's natural instinct to fall asleep on Sundays.

One memorable work-party Sunday, I turned up to collect my anglers about an hour before knocking off time and by that stage in the game the labour force were almost exhausted. They'd been working in 80° heat and they all reckoned that they had lost weight. One angler told me that one of the bailiffs had been six-foot-two when he started; he'd shrunk to five-foot-seven.

Two lorry loads of shredded tarmac had been delivered to the top end of the lake. This had to be trundled down a winding path and through two gates before it could be spread generously over the already prepared perimeter paths, but as there were only six wheelbarrows and 15 anglers had turned up to offer their services, they were operating a shift system. It worked like this; half an hour of hard graft, then a 15-minute rest followed by a 15-minute drink break.

Then there were the fag breaks and the chat breaks. In fact, there were so many breaks that it might have been better to organise a fun day out at the lake and have 15-minute work breaks. Shovelling tarmac into wheelbarrows, and out again, in what feels like high summer is thirsty work and everybody had underestimated their liquid requirements so it was handy that just up the lane there were a couple of pubs. Judging by the small mountain of empty cans, water and cola bottles, though, they were in no danger of dehydration; one of the more junior members was despatched at regular intervals to obtain cold drinks. Wisely, they chose one who didn't touch alcohol – a beer drinker with any sense would never have come back.

By lunch-time, the paths were beginning to look like the M1 and a dozen knackered anglers stood in a circle watching a couple of stalwarts finishing off the last of the tarmac, while making ribald comments including several references to builders' bums – and a whole lot worse. It had been a long day and the spectators were beginning to get that haunted look; you know the one I mean, when they're so tired they're not sure they could even squeeze in a bit of fishing. That's a scary feeling for a dedicated angler.

The wife of one of the members proudly showed me a tree that she had planted carefully on the side of a mountain of dredged-out mud on one side of the lake, in celebration of the now completed refurbishment of the complex. The sapling was about six inches high and looked like a pimple on a cow's backside but she assured me that a commemorative, two-foot-wide, brass plaque that she'd already ordered would fit eventually on the anticipated trunk. I admired the baby tree but pointed out gently, that by the time the trunk was big enough to receive this honour we'd all be dead, given that oaks take an interminable time to reach a decent size. She blinked a bit, clearly not having thought it through, but was undeterred.

The extent of the combined efforts of the morning were summed up by Cliff Kemp, co-owner of the lakes, who told me that for some strange reason he was having trouble putting on his T-shirt.
"It's really heavy," he groaned, as he wrestled with it and every muscle cried out in protest. The local chemist does a roaring trade in liniment and painkillers on work party days. It's next door to the pub.

Hypocrisy

In our small, suburban garden there was always a fair-sized blackbird, starling, and sparrow population. I had never taken much notice of them apart from expressing mild irritation, on very early summer mornings, when I was trying to write before the rest of the family surfaced from their pits, and found myself typing in time with their squawking.

One summer, a pair of robins appeared and staked out a corner of the lawn and an ivy-covered shed as their territory. I called them Robbin' and Thievin' and they were my friends; I didn't get out much in those days. They followed me around the garden, gleaning the grubs disturbed as I heaved out aliens from weed-filled borders and suddenly, because of their bare-faced cheek and friendliness, I became protective. I found myself entertaining murderous thoughts towards next-door's cat if it came within sniffing distance of my protégées, and even went so far as to steal a handful of maggots from my anglers' weekend supply to supplement the robins' diet.

I had become a hypocrite. Overnight I had turned into someone I didn't want to be. There are three things that really make me cross; injustice, pretentiousness and hypocrisy, and there I was, self-righteously prepared to feed attractive and confiding, red-breasted birds, while allowing the drab, brown and black ones to fend for themselves. It was very close to the attitude of some young men I know.

Then there was Cyril, a grey squirrel, who chattered amiably to me as I hung out the washing. If anything had happened to him I'd have been distraught, yet I have been known to cook and eat members of his family. Just the once, mind, while my boys went through a huntin', shootin' phase to accompany the fishin', and only because I was obliged, through overwhelming gratitude for the bounty they delivered to my door, to cook every single thing they ever shot, caught, found in a ditch, ran over...all right, I'm exaggerating, but it still verged on hypocrisy. Fortunately, I didn't know then what I know now. I have a monthly cookery page in Airgun World magazine and cook, eat and wax lyrical about Cyril's cousins on a regular basis. Squirrel meat is sweet and delicious, braised in white wine with shallots, mushrooms, and a little soured cream. If anyone had told me that I would become a squirrel connoisseur, I'd have been shocked.

The same hypocritical attitude applies to fish. Those who catch sea creatures have no compunction about deep-frying them, covered in batter. Try to get a carp angler to try a fillet of farmed carp, though, and they'll react as if you've offered them their pet puppy in a bap; and yet they'll eat farmed salmon or trout. I don't understand it.

Farmed carp is becoming more and more popular, locally. We have a substantial Jewish/Polish/Czech population in the town and they queue for it at our small, independent fishmonger's shop on a Saturday morning. It's only a matter of time before we'll be able to buy a variety of farmed freshwater species in supermarkets, and carp were introduced into this country in the first place as food to feed the masses. What goes around, comes around.

So, just where do we draw the line between emotional involvement and the hunter's instinct? I know a koi carp owner who lavishes attention and tender loving care upon his pets. He was horrified when I suggested jokingly that he need never leave the house because he could fish from his kitchen window. He would never even consider approaching his babies with a rod and line, he told me, and yet he spends days at a time trying to capture 'wild' species in bigger ponds. That, they tell me, is different.

Always take the weather with you

There are weekends in May when the weather is nothing short of diabolical. Often, it can be so bad that our annual air show doesn't quite take off. Oh, the planes are up there, all right, I can hear them, but as for actually seeing anything much – forget it. One year, the conditions were really dreadful. Rain and wind rattled window panes, and had birds and squirrels clinging on to trees for dear life during particularly violent gusts. It made venturing outdoors just a tad uninviting and only offered promise to those of a strange persuasion.

My family went fishing. The Chief Angler was endeavouring to keep a bivvy anchored to the ground, while he tried to outwit a decent sized carp at the same time, and the eldest, who has tendencies toward rubbing salt in wounds, went for a mile hike along an exposed sea wall. He was in search of bass, mullet, or anything else daft enough to be taking aquatic exercise, given the weather conditions.

The youngest hedged his bets and gravitated between the two, using up a whole tank of petrol in the process, while he considered which way to swing. Eventually, and sensibly in my opinion, having witnessed the suffering of his kin, he decided not to bother at all, drove home, dumped the car and walked to a nice, warm pub for a nice, cold pint.

Somebody...anybody...explain to me why they all came back blank but happy. Don't bother telling me about the youngest. I can understand why he was blank and happy, he'd had five pints, but I'd really like to know about the others. I can't make sense of it at all.

Carp virgin

I had a call from my favourite carp virgin, Elton Murphy, editor of the online fishing magazine Anglers Net, who was bivvied up at a popular water, ostensibly fishing for tench. He started off by telling me that when he'd arrived at his chosen venue, he had walked around the lake for a bit of a look, spotted Jim Gibbinson and stood back watching the master carper as he played and landed a 20lb mirror.

"Now I want one, Rosie," he said. "I've just got to get one this time. I'm tired of being a carp virgin."

I dunno, these youngsters, they want everything they see.

"Gotta go," he said. "Something's bleeping."

The following evening, there was another call. It turned out that the previous night's bleeping had been caused by the Swan family who, for reasons best known to themselves, had seemed intent on ruining

Jim Gibbinson with a 20lb 40z mirror, before the rain.

Elton's fishing career. Despite his feathered friends, he was jubilant and told me that he had at last lost his cherry to a fine 17lb mirror.

I received a blow-by-blow account of how his deflowering had taken place. My hero had seen the carp break surface and had cast toward it, not holding out too much hope, but while he was busy concentrating on re-baiting his other rods, all hell broke loose as the surfacing fish made a run for it.

I could have told him this would happen, had he asked me. In all my years of carp angling observation, I couldn't fail to note that carp have a slapstick sense of humour. I have witnessed, first hand, their ability to get the timing exactly right and then revel in causing as much disruption as they possibly can. You can't blame them; it must be pretty boring just swimming about all day, looking for food, mating once a year and doing the occasional poo.

Elton had been worried about landing his first carp. He'd already lost a biggish one from this same spot a few weeks earlier, and to accompany that psychological barrier he had the disadvantage of using a new and therefore unfamiliar rod. However, newly purchased bite alarms that he had left out in solid rain for 36 hours didn't let him down and neither did the bait, which was The Remedy from Mistral. I told you it was blow-by-blow! He gave me all the details, a couple of times over, including the size of the hook, but I've forgotten that. This all happened a few years ago, you understand, and The Remedy is no longer available from Mistral, although I'm told that they've replaced it with something equally magnificent.

The weather, over the couple of days that Elton had chosen for his quest, had started off okay, but was beginning to show signs of a predicted hurricane and worsening by the minute. I could hear the sound of heavy rain hitting the canvas of his bivvy and a force eight gale whipping the sides.

"You all right?" I asked, concerned about his welfare.

"Not really, Rosie," he replied and then described, in heart-rending tones, just how wet it was, both inside the bivvy and out.

"It seems as if the lake is trying to get into my bivvy," he said. "There's at least an inch of water on the floor of it and everything I brought with me is soaking wet.

Bit of a storm brewing!

I've got no dry clothes to change into and I don't know where to put my sleeping bag. My bedchair is so old and saggy that my bum touches the floor when I lie on it."

I told him that he should think himself lucky. My bum does that on a brand new bedchair, and it's no fault of the chair, unfortunately.

I felt sorry for him. The poor boy was cold, very damp, and worried about how he was going to cope during the night. As he was speaking, he poured himself a cup of hot coffee from his Thermos and the relief in his voice as he sipped this wonderful restorative got my maternal instinct going. Sometimes I wish I didn't have one. It rears up when I see animals in distress, too.

"Oh, dear," I sympathised, ready to rush off to Kent with warm fluffy towels and hot soup if need be. "Hold on a minute, though. There is a clubhouse, isn't there? If conditions get too dire, you could always retire there for the night. At least you'll be dry."

"I can't do that!" exclaimed my friend. "What about me rods? I can't leave them. It's against angling law."

"Well, take 'em with you, then," says I, without thinking. Silly mare, I really should have known better.

"What?" cried Elton in disbelief at my stupidity. "and lose the chance of catching another carp? Not likely!"

I phoned him the following morning. He had spent a blank, moist and uncomfortable night but became considerably moister every time he thought about that mirror, he told me. I found out afterwards that

Elton, no longer a virgin, in fine drizzle with a 17lb mirror.

the monsoon conditions had eased up for about four minutes, sufficiently and just long enough for Elton to land and photograph his prize, but it wouldn't have mattered if the rain and wind had been at storm force. I should have known that he'd be a willing victim, that he'd risk drowning, catching a chill - or worse - all in vain anticipation of the capture of a decent fish. It's what anglers do.

CHAPTER SIX

FLAMING JUNE

Terminal boredom

Sometimes, despite the frenetic preparation, nervous breakdowns over the weather forecast and desperate bait collection, the fishing aboard a charter boat is so slow that terminal boredom sets in. The anglers are captive in anticlimax. There's no turning back because, by the time they find out that the day is going to be unproductive, the tide has gone out and they're stuck with it, for at least eight hours.

After one particularly blank session, I had the temerity to ask them what they did all day, adrift in an open boat with no outside stimulation. I could imagine them all staring at the horizon waiting for the momentary relief of a passing ship, a rocky outcrop, or a sudden storm; anything to break up the monotony. They wouldn't admit to anything directly, but you can gather a vast amount of information just by listening to conversations during the after-trip drinking session, especially if you're the one who remains sober because you've got to drive them all home. I used to find that the best time to extract any information was after their fourth pint.

When they get really fed up, apparently, they indulge in a form of spectator athletics. Whelk races or hermit crab hurdling are popular events and the foredeck takes on the ambience of Ascot, or more likely Newmarket, since the hats worn aren't exactly the height of fashion. The unfortunate, and probably unwilling, participants in these events are given names, usually reflecting a distinguishing feature of their respective anatomies, before being lined up, pointed in the direction of the winning post and urged on raucously by their trainers. I wouldn't be at all surprised to discover that the winner is paraded round the deck in a lap of honour.

The crabs are caught accidentally, being the only sea creatures on these occasions to be tempted by

carefully prepared strips of herring intended for greater species, and on very rare occasions, accompanied by squeals of delight, a lobster may be hauled in. An angler in the throes of terminal ennui is a pretty awesome sight and should be avoided at all costs, so whelks are dredged up deliberately by the skipper because the poor bloke has to entertain his party somehow, and most skippers can't sing.

There is one cardinal rule. No matter how bad it gets, they don't play with the bait supply. Ragworm or soft-backed crabs are protected from potential marauding practical jokers. You never know if the fish may yet partake of a light luncheon, and if a ragworm is knackered from being forced to hurtle down the straight, it's not going to do its job properly.

One of the many excuses given by anglers for a day out sea fishing is that they only go for your sake, so that you can eat fresh fish for no outlay or effort on your part. They conveniently forget the cost of a mountain of food that has to be provided, prepared and transported to the boat to sustain them as they suffer on your behalf, coupled with the exorbitant price of double-strength paracetamol and/or chocolate that becomes a vital part of any fishing widow's existence.

They will tell you that they expend large amounts of energy in concentrating on bringing home the bacon, or more likely a bedraggled codling, but we know that they sit there wasting their time with childish and time-consuming activities. To add insult to injury, they bet on the results. You can always spot the winner. He's the one with so much loose change in his right-hand pocket that he lists to starboard as he makes his way to the nearest pub after the trip.

The gambling continues, even when the lure of crab and whelk racing has lost its charm. They have been known to play a form of Pooh-sticks. This is a game of pure chance as far as I can see, although they insist there's a certain amount of skill involved. They all crowd to one side of the boat and yell at chosen pieces of flotsam, one per angler, in much the same way as they screamed encouragement at crabs and whelks, but downwards. The piece of debris, floating in the current, which arrives at the prow of the boat first, is declared the winner.

Charter boats at rest.

When all other forms of entertainment have been exhausted, card schools are set up and if they've run out of money, they'll bet with small bits and pieces of tackle. This usually resulted in me paying a special visit to the tackle shop before the next weekend trip, in order to replace the lost items. My anglers were notoriously bad card-players.

Toward the end of the day out, they play with the ship's radio. Winding up other skippers in the near vicinity begins when they cast off and has been known to continue for hours but when it's nearly home time, the airwave activity is increased. The protagonists always go too far with the 'good-natured' insults, and this often provokes small, 'good-natured' scuffles wharf-side when the boats moor up in the late evening. Some of these spats are 'too much alcohol through boredom' induced and have been known to draw blood, and a small crowd shouting encouragement.

In the summer months, when all else fails to grab their attention, they drink the day's allotment of beer within a couple of hours and then fall asleep, either half-naked and flat on the deck where they achieve that toasted look by the end of the day, or sitting semi-prone on bedchairs. In the latter position, too much sun on a rippled beer gut makes a stomach take on a Venetian blind effect and is extremely painful, apparently. I was once commanded to 'stop moving', by the CA, as I walked past his armchair, en route to the kitchen because anything remotely stirring his air space was causing excruciating pain.

During winter voyages, they sleep in the same positions, but for obvious reasons encase themselves in flotation suits, thermal underwear, balaclavas, and gauntlets. They still achieve a kind of tan, even in the direst conditions; it's called windburn.

So, when they come home empty-handed, considerably out of pocket and with tales of a hard and unsuccessful day at sea, don't you believe it.

On a slow day, even the Martello towers look interesting.

Dedicated followers of fashion

The first fortnight of June used to be spent gearing up towards the night of the fifteenth. Come the glorious day, my anglers would arrive at the lake mid-afternoon and sit chatting for hours, exchanging anecdotes, bait recipes and new rigs they intended to try out the minute midnight was upon them. New baits, finely tuned after much experimentation sat waiting for the off; tackle was bright, shiny, and ready to go.

There they'd sit like coiled springs in anticipation of the witching hour when they could cast out for the first time in the new freshwater fishing season. The excitement was almost tangible and, strangely, it happens to a degree even now when the lakes have been open all year. Old habits die hard and that seems to be one that endures, even now when there is no need for it. It almost makes up for the other superficial and fleeting 'fashions' that take over the angling scene from time to time.

I suspect that you may already be aware of these crazes, being angling orientated, but I had never noticed them until a fellow fishing widow pointed out the fad aspect of fishing to me. The more I thought about it, the more I discovered that she was right; there are trends. Everyone seems to go mad for something for one season, and then by the following year, that's all forgotten and something else comes along that must be used/acquired.

I don't mean the very small number of anglers who want to look trendy. Oh yes, there are a few, and I've seen the desire to be fashionable overtake the good taste of certain anglers of my acquaintance at a difficult time in their lives, i.e. male menopause. I've even seen one really sad man wearing a gold medallion on the outside of his babygro; it's true, I promise you! Never mind 'Back to the Future'; 'back to the 80s' was more like it. Gold tooth flashing, and a huge golden chain with what looked like one of those chocolate coins you give the kids at Christmas attached to it. I was thankful he wasn't sporting chest hair, but I did wonder who on earth he was trying to impress.

One season, in our neck of the woods, it was all fruit flavours for bait, and they used the real McCoy because the passion for fruit happened to coincide with the soft fruit season. It was hand-made, too; mashed into fishmeal, topped up with a drip or two of bottled flavouring and some sweetener, and then fashioned into boilies. I couldn't see the point. Why not just buy existing fruit-flavoured bait if they were going to stuff it full of chemical flavouring, anyway?

There was one year when my boys were still at school when making homemade carp mats out of cornflake packets and sticky-backed plastic (not really, I made that bit up) was a trend. If you're really hard up and can't afford to buy a proper unhooking mat, an old, soft canvas jacket with the sleeves cut off, sewn around the edges and stuffed with sheet foam makes a good substitute until you can persuade your mother to buy you one. I swear there was a contest for who could wear their mother down the quickest. My boys always seemed to win.

The following year though, fads moved toward hemp juice in groundbait, home produced fishmeal and hemp boilies, with whisky to flavour – real whisky, I ask you! What a waste of good Scotch; and in order to achieve hempishness, let's ruin the wife's only decent, Christmas pudding-sized, aluminium saucepan, which had cost a whole fiver in 1976, with piggin' hemp seed. Have you seen what hemp can do to the innards of a favourite kitchen utensil? Black as your hat, it ends up, or covered in grey scum if it hasn't yet been used continually.

"What are you making so much fuss about?" I was chided when I made loud, but according to those who know these things, unnecessary complaint about the smell produced by boiling the stuff. "It's only a herb."

Is it? Really? Then why is it illegal to possess or partake of large amounts of one of hemp's distant cousins? Since when has it been against the law to smoke sage, thyme, or basil? Mind you, maybe you hemp enthusiasts should produce cannabis-flavoured boilies. In fact, the more I think about it, the more sensible the whole thing becomes. You would be able to catch a carp with a snack-sized Mars bar or a packet of cheese and onion crisps; they'd be too busy giggling to put up much of a fight or worry about hooks - not that I know anything about it, obviously. Oh, I see. That's where the idea breaks down, isn't it? That's why no one has thought of it before. You don't want carp to surrender willingly, that'd take all the fun out of it. Go on then, ruin another saucepan. It'll all change next season, anyway.

Rats!

One of the bailiffs at the club water told me that he had arrived for his early morning stint only to be greeted by hundreds, so he said, of basking snakes. I suspect it was more likely a couple of dozen but I let him get away with it; he's an angler and prone to exaggeration, after all.

"They had got their little heads in the bushes, and had left their bodies strewn over the paths, basking in the early morning sun."

Was he frightened?

"Too right," he said. "I made as much noise as I could and stamped my feet, until they disappeared."

What a tart!

I felt so much better after I had heard his tale. It reminded me of an incident a few years ago when I had been asked to give number one son a lift to the club. He had persuaded me to give him a hand, one summer afternoon, to carry the vast amount of equipment necessary for his comfort during a long night session and I have been ashamed of my cowardice ever since. It's comforting to know that a grown man, an experienced out-of-doors bailiff, can feel trepidation too.

There is an abundance of wildlife at the lake including rats. Rats with a capital Rer.

"It's okay," I was told by the prospective night angler. "They're not aggressive."

That was hardly surprising, given their standard of living. They are huge, well fed and arrogant; I can imagine them calmly attempting to unscrew vacuum flasks and rummaging through sandwiches, selecting the ones with the most succulent fillings, then strolling off with them without a by your leave or a thank you. I was expected to leave my first-born here all night, without a whimper of protest. He'd have just a canvas bivvy and a torch for protection against these super-rats.

"Don't worry, Ma," he said, trying to reassure me as we trudged the half-mile round the lake, fully laden. "There won't be any rats here yet, they usually come out at dusk. Watch out for the adders, though."

"Adders? What as in snakes, do you mean?"

He gave me one of his pitying 'what a shame you're only a girly' looks. "I don't mean maths students. It's all right. They don't come out during the day."

He had noted the horror on my face and was lying through his teeth in case I flipped and made him go home again.

"What about at night? You said they come out at night. You'll be here all night!" Gibbering mode had set in; he was totally unperturbed.

I became increasingly nervous and couldn't bear to watch while he set up. He didn't give me a backward glance as I hurtled through undergrowth toward the car park making enough noise to startle anything, rat or adder, which may have been in my path. Next time he wanted a hand I made his brother go with him.

Death in the morning

Speaking of rats made me think of something almost completely unconnected, a tenuous link being the reason that the eldest kept an old Webley Tempest air pistol buried deep in his tackle box. It was all above board, he was a member of the BASC, a shooting club, and was trusted to be a responsible young man. The lake owner was aware that he had the Webley and had sanctioned the use of it for the disposal of rats, providing there were no other anglers on the complex at the time. It was used rarely but effectively during an occasional difference of opinion with an over-sized, marauding, snack-seeking rat in the wee, small hours of the night but the pistol was more for a feeling of security than for intended use.

One morning, I had gone to collect him from the lake at a prearranged time, and decided not to comment on his unusually quiet demeanour. Not a word passed his lips during the 20-minute journey home but I reasoned that if I'd been camped out in the kind of weather he'd been stuck in over the past few days, I wouldn't feel like making jolly conversation, either.

Silence reigned as he unpacked the car, as he dumped all the gear in the hallway, as he flung dirty clothes in the general vicinity of the washing machine. Questions about his health, appetite, and plans for the rest of the day were ignored.

There he stood; the hunter home from the hill, or as near to a hill as you can get in Essex. His usual routine was food, a hot bath and a couple of hours kip so when that ravenous body stayed stationary, instead of adopting its more usual, hands outstretched, mouth open, bee-line kitchenwards, I knew that there was something seriously amiss.

It turned out that he'd had to shoot a rabbit. He told me that he had gone for a walk around at first light, checking for signs of carp on the feed, and had come face to face with a pathetic creature sitting in the middle of one of the paths. He was not amused when I interrupted to ask if it had been Mick, one of the lake's bailiffs, and I wished I had held my flippant tongue as he continued his sorry tale.

Broken-voiced, he went on to tell me that it had been a rabbit. One of the scores of myxamatosis victims among the local bunny population, most of the fur on the poor creature's head had been scratched away, its eyes were blind and bulging with pus and mucus and, almost a skeleton covered in scabs and sores, it sat quivering, awaiting death.

The eldest, a strapping 22-year old at the time, had tears in his eyes. He'd had no choice, he explained, but to collect his air pistol and shoot it; the rabbit's suffering was too distressing to contemplate leaving it there to die in agony. He vehemently declined the tentative, and badly timed, offer of breakfast and instead walked to the home of the lake owner to report his action and to discuss some way of alleviating the plight of the affected colony. They closed the complex for a day and organised a cull. It was the only thing to do. The situation was dealt with efficiently and humanely but it was several days before number one son managed to work up enough enthusiasm to go fishing again.

A matter of life and death

After a family bereavement and anticipating celebrations with yet another empty chair at festive tables, the last thing I wanted was to dwell on the transience of life and the loss of loved ones, but sometimes it's difficult not to let the mind wander and I was in philosophical mood when my phone rang. It was a mate who urged me to telephone a mutual friend asap.

"He's lost ALL his beloved perch, Rosie," came a sympathetic cry from the heart for our friend's distress. "Every single one of 'em. Dead. Choked on maggots, they did! You've just got to ring him and offer words of comfort."

"Poor thing," I said consolingly, but a tad insincerely. As a general rule, fish do not leave empty spaces at dining tables. "He must be distraught. Can't he get some more?"

"Of course not! How long have you been on the fishing scene? Don't you know it's illegal? He inherited those perch with the house and the pond. There's no way he can replace them."

Dutifully, I phoned to offer my condolences a few days later and the bereaved one's wife answered the phone. I asked her what had happened and she told me that there's a family habit of decanting leftover baits into the pond after every fishing trip.

"That's fine, in the summer," Helen told me, "but this time of the year when the temperature drops, any food chucked in the pond just poisons the water because the fish aren't feeding, except for the perch, so we don't usually do it."

On this occasion, though, due to certain angling brains on automatic pilot, this is exactly what had happened. Superfluous maggots were thrown unthinkingly into the pond, and the perch, being greedy little devils, sucked up the whole lot, couldn't digest the excess and choked to death.

I'm afraid I laughed when Helen told me that any mention of the P word (perch) or baits other than boilies caused her husband to wince painfully. The family were treading very carefully about his bruised psyche, reminiscent of Basil Fawlty and 'don't mention the war.'

It made me think, though, for although fish do not leave gaps at family gatherings, they do in the hearts of men. Five years previously, when our club water's biggest carp died, there was much weeping, wailing and gnashing of teeth, bowed heads and, stiff upper lips. Club members even held a cringe-worthy funeral and erected a small headstone in honour of the dear departed. I didn't understand it at all; it's a fish, for goodness sake, not somebody's mother!

Big Scale. Caught by accident in 1987

Apparently, though, the carp obsession grabs some anglers so deeply that they will give up everything in order to catch a

RIP.

particular specimen. When I say 'everything' I mean job, house, car, family life, marriage, contact with their kids…and they are proud of their sacrifice, as if a destiny beyond their control impels them to go without so much, for the sake of a carp. So when these creatures die, it's almost as if a family member has shuffled off this mortal coil and their grief is real. Recently, some of the biggest, best loved, and most caught carp in the country have died and on the Internet forums, there were declarations of eternal devotion. Messages of love and respect are addressed directly to the fish – as if they can read now they're dead. It makes little sense to me, but we're all different and who am I to judge? I wouldn't hurt a living thing – except wasps – but I'm not an animal lover per se, apart from a plateful of roast lamb on a Sunday; I love that!

The eldest was gutted when I told him about Big Scale. The capture of this carp by accident when he was 14, he was fishing for tench at the time, had been his introduction to carp fishing nearly 12 years before and he hadn't looked back. Gradually, from that day onward, he became a proficient carp angler. Dave was not alone in his feelings of loss. Every angler to whom I spoke said the same thing; it was like losing an old friend, they said.

The last person to hook Big Scale, a youngster who had caught the fish at 31lb 6oz, said a few words at the requiem mass and reported that the carp had seemed to be in good health when he'd landed it. There didn't appear to be any reason for its demise, apart from age. Forty years was a rough estimate but most folk considered the carp to be much older than that.

Big Scale's final captor worked for a stonemason. He found a piece of scrap marble, cut it to shape and lovingly, made a small headstone in memory of a fish that had given many anglers a great deal of pleasure and excitement.

I have to say that I found myself caught up in it all and hypocritically, put a few wild flowers on the headstone when I thought of it and there was nothing better to do at the lake. This was in the days when I was not allowed to join in with the fishing, and there are only so many blackberries you can gather before tedium sets in. Big Scale, no doubt about it, had made quite an impact on others too, as well as number one son who had caught the fish twice in five years. Dave had been inspired enough to write an article for Carpworld magazine, way back in 1994*, about this beloved carp. In fact, you could say that Big Scale, and the kindness of Tim Paisley, launched his writing career. It was the first article he ever had published, written from the heart and makes excellent reading because of it. * See Appendix

I had assumed that it was just carp that inspired such grief, but now it seemed that perch was also a contender. So I really did sympathise with Barry being completely perchless, when I'd had time to think it through. Nothing lasts, though, does it? Nothing ever stays the same. There will always be other fish, and other people, who take a step up the ladder when there's a death at the top; it's the one thing we can be sure of. We're all going to end up the same way. Best get out there fishing while you can!

Weed problems

The downside of introducing your girlfriend to carp fishing, I was told by a young friend, is that she will assume full knowledge after the capture of just one carp.

There's more than one type of weed problem!

"Why do women do that?" he complained. "I don't pretend to know everything about cookery just because I've made a piece of toast!"

"I'd hooked into a small crucian," he went on, "and the other half was not interested at all. She kept telling me it was a clump of weed."

She could tell, apparently, by looking at the bend in the rod. She had just caught her first carp and had instantly become an expert. She knew about these things and it definitely looked like weed, therefore it was. End of.

"I'd been playing it for about 15 minutes," he said, still disgruntled and suffering from a lack of attention. "She surely couldn't imagine that I was daft enough to continue if it was a lump of weed, for goodness sake!"
"'How big was it?" I asked him.
"Oh, about the size of a...erm...a clump of weed, actually," he replied.

Well, there you are then. She was half right.

The f words

Football, food and fishing, that's all they think about, and not necessarily in that order. "All right if I have a few mates round for a footy afternoon?" asked number one son as the World Cup season gathered momentum, and the weather was too wet and windy to sit by a water's edge, with any degree of sanity.

I agreed with the request. His father was fishing and likely to stay at the lake until dark, around 9pm; the Chief Angler's sanity had been in question for many years, particularly if fishing was involved. There was nothing on TV that didn't have a ball in it anyway until early evening, when the detective series that I wanted to view was due to be broadcast. All the youngsters would have returned to their respective homes by then, wouldn't they?

I should have known better. It was my own fault for not setting the parameters beforehand. They arrived in good time for the first match, mid-morning, and made hungry noises about 1pm, so I fed them, stupid woman. After the match, they sat flicking through a few fishing videos, John Wilson, Matt Hayes, Chris Ball, turned over to Sky TV for Rex Hunt and more Matt Hayes, by which time it was kick-off for the afternoon football session.

One of my guests disappeared briefly at about 6pm-ish. Great, I thought; one down, seven to go. He returned after about ten minutes with an armful of fragrant fish and chip parcels which were dispensed among the undernourished and received as if they hadn't devoured three French sticks, a pound of cheese, two dozen packets of crisps and several chocolate bars a few hours previously.

The food go-getter had also had the presence of mind to go to his own house and collect another couple of fishing videos to watch until kick-off for the last match of the day, so I ended up retreating to the bedroom and watching my mediocre detective thriller on a set with wobbly knobs and an even dodgier picture. I began to hate football, possibly fishing, and occasionally teenaged boys with obsessive personalities.

It paid off, though. Nearly all those lads, now grown with families of their own, keep in touch with me and reminisce about what fun it used to be in our house. Bless 'em.

CHAPTER SEVEN

JULY-KIT HOT?

In denial

The Chief Angler used to have regular holidays; conger fishing, shark hunting, trout or salmon catching, carp capturing...you name it. I had no problem with him going away without me; in fact, it was like a holiday for me when he did. For a whole seven days, I could do exactly as I pleased with no recriminations for lack of obedience.

There were no shirts to wash and iron. I could eat my favourite meals, egg and chips, steamed fish in parsley sauce, and anything else frowned upon by the CA as 'not proper dinners.' I could play my piano or listen to CDs at eardrum-shattering volume with no fear of my anti-social behaviour interfering with Sport TV and generally behave in an unruly and undisciplined manner until he came back and demanded a return to normal routine. I had absolutely no qualms about being left on my own; I looked forward to it.

What puzzled me was his attitude towards these slices of fishing adventure, and he's not alone. I've spoken to other anglers who think the same way. There were occasions when he became stressed at work and complained that he needed a holiday. When I pointed out that he'd already had three 'holidays' that year so another one wouldn't make any difference to me, he told me that this was not so. 'They weren't holidays!' he exclaimed, horrified that I should accuse him of having a good time. 'They were just fishing trips.'

The fact that these breaks away from home were spent in pastures new, in congenial company, staying in hotels with evening entertainment, abundant good food prepared by someone else, and his days spent doing what he loved best, fishing, didn't appear to be relevant. Sounded pretty much like a holiday to me!

Trouble is, a vacation without fishing doesn't appear to be an option. One summer, with time on my hands and the boys grown-up and old enough to look after themselves, I suggested that we take off for a few days with no particular destination in mind.
"We could find a B & B somewhere," I said. "Explore the countryside, visit old buildings, take long walks, pub lunches…"
"Great idea," was his response. "We'll just throw the fishing gear in the car and go!"

I gave up. If he thought I was going to drive 500 miles, squished up in a car full of fishing gear, he could think again. Even driving to our local lake was a feat of endurance surrounded by the amount of stuff he considered essential, let alone sufficient equipment to meet every eventuality on unfamiliar waters.

You may think I was being unreasonable but I'd had previous experience to call upon. We only had one holiday together in 30 years, and most of that was spent apart. In 1984, I was researching my first book and needed to visit the Somerset village where my great-grandmother was born, so I booked a week's bed and breakfast on a pig farm. I didn't choose a pig-farm specifically, you understand; unfortunately, we didn't discover what kind of farm it was until we arrived. The week was doomed before it began despite the farmer's wife assuring us that we would get used to the unholy stench. We didn't; it takes more than a week, I'm telling you!

The Chief Angler and our eldest son spent most of their time visiting tackle shops and sitting beside the River Parrett, trying to tempt large chub while waiting for me, and an extremely bored seven-year-old, to return from trolling around record offices and old churches, to pick them up. I only forgot where I'd left them once, and that wasn't all due to my lack of navigational skill. Some of it was, I admit. The lanes, stiles and 'landmark' cottages of Somerset all looked the same to me and I must have driven at least a dozen extra miles trying to find the right spot. I did find it eventually; only to discover that they had walked on an extra half mile 'to a better stretch of the river' from where I'd deposited them several hours earlier. I was greeted with 'Where've you been! We're hungry!' How was I supposed to know where they were in the days before mobile phones?

The couple of long weekends spent in Brixham while Himself and his mates were conger hunting didn't count as holidays, for me, either. The youngest and I spent most of the time on our own and might just as well have been at home, in comfort, instead of roaming around the Torbay Riviera all day, until it was time to wander down to the wharf, late evening, to await the arrival of the charter-boat. We tried to join in but the anglers, who were too knackered from hauling congers all day to be bothered with socialising, just wanted to collapse in the bar, hold a verbal action replay on the day's events and then, when they couldn't possibly force any more alcohol down their necks, 'have an early night because we're out at 5am.' I couldn't wait to get home to sweet-smelling clothes and a room which didn't contain unwashed fishing tackle/clothes and vodka/lager fumes, not to mention...well, best I don't mention the other fumes.

Conger, crab and lobster...

This 'it's not a holiday' condition appears to be hereditary, too. The eldest, editor of a sea-angling magazine, sea fishes and writes about it for a living. What does he do for recreation? I'll give you one guess; he goes freshwater angling. Sometimes, he'll go for a week in the company of fishing mates, either to France on a carp trip, or for a few days bivvied up on an English water in search of anything that'll

...but they're not on holiday!

co-operate. The latter, I can relate to, by the way. Over the past 12 months, or so, I've spent weekends in a bivvy, in the company of close friends, enjoyed myself immensely and emerged feeling relaxed and mentally refreshed, almost as if I've been on holiday, in fact! Dave insists that his solitary, weeklong diversions from the daily grind are not holidays, though. They're 'just fishing.' I blame his father.

So, maybe the Chief Angler had a point. I didn't enjoy my 'fishing holiday as a family' experiences; more like hard work than a welcome break, I reckon. Perhaps that's how anglers see these weeks away, but then if it's so demanding, why do they do it so often? I don't know or even pretend to understand.

Holiday washday blues

The summer holidays when your anglers are youngsters can be hard work, and I used to dread the last week in July in anticipation of the following six weeks of school holiday. I always seemed to be surrounded by kids. My sons were very popular and their friends appeared to live in our house for the full duration. Not that I minded that much, but it would have been nice if someone else's mum had entertained my boys for a day, now and again. It was hard work at times.

To be the ideal angler's mum, you'd have to be one of those women who are capable of organising and completing the housework before 9am, having already fed a family of four, plus dog, with kedgeree, devilled kidneys, homemade just-baked rolls and freshly-squeezed orange juice.

There are such women. A friend told me that apart from the pre-dawn onslaught against dust and grime, every evening she prepares the next morning's breakfasts, vegetables for the evening meal, loads the washing machine with the day's dirty laundry and lays out fresh clothing for the family to put on the following morning. I'd be laid out for the rest of the week, makes me tired just thinking about it.

Her frenetic lifestyle began during one school summer holiday, so that at the drop of a hat she could be ready to join in with her youngsters as they pursued their fishing activities. It became a habit and she is now totally organised at all times. I admired her greatly, but I know my own limitations. There was no way I could ever compete.

This wonder-woman accompanied her kids on fishing trips, bait-digging sessions, even sat on convenient logs while they stalked carp or played pike - in all weathers, for goodness sake. I wondered, but never had the courage to ask, how they felt about her looking over their shoulders all the time. I know that my own boys would have done their utmost to get me out of their way.

Mind you, her family co-operated by rigidly keeping to the house rules. There had to be a strict routine or the whole system would fall apart. I know. Inspired by example, I tried it for two whole days before we all became thoroughly fed up with the regimentation. I only managed to enforce two of the basic regulations and for the benefit of those fishing mums, who think it must be worth a try, these are they:

Firstly, you should ensure that they empty their own pockets, particularly if they've just returned from fishing, just in case there is something still living and lurking in a zipped compartment; I've been caught out by maggots, bloodworms and assorted grubs, ragworm and mussels, on occasion. You should be aware that clothes-washing sessions after a fishing trip might contain hidden hazards. Apart from the squillion hooks and weights that spew out of unzipped pockets, there could be other little surprises.

One nasty shock I sustained was a small, brown rabbit's foot that jumped out of my front loader and grabbed me by the throat. When I screamed up the stairs for assistance (I had the sense, by the way, to give my sons two syllable names. It adds a bit of momentum to the voice when trying to screech over 60 watts of heavy metal) I was told that it was a 'lucky' rabbit's foot, part of the young angler's essential equipment, to be carried at all times. Yes, I blow dried it and handed it back, neatly coiffured.

Following up as a close second in the rigid code of behaviour, are boots. You must insist, when they return exhausted and weary from wherever they've been, and it could be merely a trip to the local corner shop for a couple of Mars bars, that they deal with their own boots. If not sorted out immediately, they will be kicked off in the garden to lie gradually decomposing until the next time they are needed. It may rain in the meantime and when the boots are needed urgently, their owners will suffer a panic attack and a hair-drier will be thrust into the toes in an attempt to dry them out in a hurry. Hair-driers explode through overheating in about seven minutes. Of course, an organised mum would grab the boots before they muddied the hall carpet. They would be whisked away, cleaned, polished, and put away ready for their next outing, thus saving the expense of a new hair-drier.

I knew it all made sense but I'm just not one of those wondrous women. Slap-dash is still my middle name and housework was the bane of my life. I'm an excellent cook but vacuuming and dusting I can do without, and a washer I'm not, unless you don't mind your clothes being shredded, faded, stretched, or accidentally tie-dyed. The daily wash was sorted, after a fashion, whites roughly separated from coloureds, but accidents would happen and my family became resigned to the fact that there was a good chance they might never again see their favourite garments in their pre-washed condition.

My excuse is that I was usually preoccupied and in a hurry to get things over and done with, so anything that looked vaguely like fishing clothes was forced into the machine in one go. They had to go on the 'Whites, Heavy Soil' cycle, there was just no other way to shift the unidentifiable stains, but there was one advantage to my washing methods, the youngest never had to wear hand-me-downs. There was nothing left to hand down after I'd washed it a few times.

Plumbing the depths

It's not a good idea to head lakewards suffering from a surfeit of lager. One Sunday, at closing time, I drove a car full of fishing gear and a large picnic down to the local pub, collected Himself from the snug where he had spent several hours in convivial company, and transported the lot to the lake where Simon, the youngest, and girlfriend had been set up for half a day.

On one of the lakes there was a roped off area, out of casting bounds to the anglers and provided so the carp had a fighting chance of a bit of peace and quiet. They could run away and hide in this sanctuary when they became fed up with it all.

The anglers, who fished the swim adjacent to the roped off bit, always tried to get as close as they could to it, hoping for a stiff breeze which might carry their bait just under the rope. Not very sporting really, but anglers will be anglers.

It took the lager lout a good hour to tackle up, the memory cells misfire after a certain number of pints, but eventually, he was up and running and cast out to the very edge of the ropes. He reckoned the alcohol intake enhanced his aim and he was so accurate that the rig touched the rope, twizzled around it, somehow tied itself into a knot and stayed there.

"Gotta get that back," I heard him mutter." That's the only decent rig I've got with me."

Knowing from experience that the CA didn't do 'going in the water to get stuff' and it was usually down to me, I began to remove my sandals in readiness. It didn't take long; it was a very hot day and I was already wearing the minimum amount of clothing for decency, a cotton dress and knickers, to be exact. I'd soon dry off in the sun.

"You stay put," said the youngest, ever protective of his mother. "I'll go if I have to but we could try and get it with a rod. It's not far out and it's not hooked, only wound round the rope."

By the time they had finished messing about, they had lost the rod tip to the rope as well. Someone would have to enter the water and I'd already been told that it wouldn't be me. Wearing his only pair of work boots and colourful Bermuda shorts, the youngest strolled in to retrieve. We thought most of the fish would disappear to the other end of the lake, if only to get away from the glare reflected off his white legs which only see the light of day on hot, summer Sundays, but an hour after the successful rescue attempt, the Chief Angler caught two fine carp within 40 minutes of each other. The reason, he told me, was that he had noted the fact that our boy had only been drenched from toe to mid-thigh.

"I thought it was deeper than that," he said. "So I adjusted the hook length. Good job he went in, really, wasn't it?"

Well, no it wasn't, actually. You try getting a pair of heavy-duty, leather work boots dry in 12 hours or so. Despite being placed upside down on a bank of dried mud for the rest of the day, looking as if someone had dived in head-first, and placed on the floor of the airing cupboard on reaching home, they still weren't dried out by the following morning. The boy had to wear his best, black leather, nightclub lace-ups to work which came home covered in solder; at the time, Simon was an electronics engineer with no sense of direction.

I thanked my son for taking my place in the rig rescue and promised to replace his two sets of ruined footwear. "I didn't mind," he said, "and it was worth it so Dad could get those carp." I gave up.

Out for a duck

It seems that plumbing the depths of a water efficiently can be a good idea. I had never really understood why this time-consuming task should be necessary until I was told this little tale by a young and inexperienced angler. He wishes to remain anonymous because, he told me, he felt a big enough prat on the day and would rather not broadcast his identity so that the whole country is aware of his slip-up.

The youngster had cast out carefully about 70 yards and sat down to await developments. He'd been sitting there

Ducks waiting to take the pee.

for 20 minutes watching several families of ducks swimming back and forth just in front of his bait, when one of them stood up. It turned out that they were all swimming in about four inches of water over a sandbar and our novice had either missed it completely when plumbing, or hadn't the required experience to interpret when the lead hit the bottom. He was so embarrassed, he said, just in case any other 'proper' carpers in nearby swims had seen his error that he packed up and moved to the other end of the lake to start afresh. Bless!

Good morning campers!

Most fishing widows who have young anglers in the family view the six weeks of school summer holidays with alarm; it wasn't just me, I'm sure. The juniors want to go fishing all day, every day, and develop an attitude when you try to explain that household chores have to be done first. It is just not possible to drop everything, rush out at dawn, return at dusk, and expect the fairies to have washed clothes, cooked meals, and tidied up during your absence.

Nothing changes as they grow older, believe me, apart from the fact that they no longer rely on you for transport and they definitely don't want to have you tagging along. For a while, your priority will be paying for driving lessons and financing their first car. They'll want to go on a fishing holiday with their friends, without an adult in tow and you have to bite your tongue, sit on your hands, and let them go. How else are they going to find out how to be adults?

For financial reasons, the first few times will be camping jobs. They'll tell you not to worry; they are hard, they are men. He, of the cushy number: food prepared, laundry done, bed made, hot water on tap, free telephone…is going to have to fend for himself, on a beach/in a field for a whole week. "Piece of cake," he told me, shrugging off the dire warnings of being cold at night, hungry by day, tired through trying to sleep in unfamiliar surroundings and having to shave in his morning tea.

Early one misty morning, they set off for the wilds of Wales; four hulking great young men in a small Fiesta with enough equipment to see them through a nuclear disaster. The tents were stowed in a roof rack container, together with four huge rucksacks and a crate of tinned food purloined from the store cupboards of four households.

Water containers were forced into the boot, empty after I casually mentioned that they might save a drop of petrol if they filled them on arrival at their destination, rather than cart eight gallons of southern rainfall 300 miles, or so. Rods and reels were cuddled all the way to Anglesey.

The remote field toward which they were heading belonged to a farmer who was the cousin of an aunt by marriage of a friend's friend. Hardly a close connection but they spoke of him as if they'd known him for years; everything was going to be 'wicked'. They couldn't wait to get away from the monotony of three hot meals a day and a solid roof over their heads.

Two days later, after 6pm, there was a reversed charge telephone call from North Wales. They'd run out of money, food and couldn't seem to tempt the carp. They were sick of Kendal Mint Cake, they said, and they'd be home tomorrow evening. It was suggested, forcibly, that I go shopping first thing in the morning for the ingredients to construct a huge steak and kidney pie, with chips accompaniment, to be ready and instantly accessible the moment they staggered through the front door toward the kitchen. They were starving, they said, and probably wouldn't have any clothes that fitted by the time they came back. They'd used all the fuel for the Porta-gas cooker and all they had was a loaf of bread and some cheese, which they'd managed to buy with loose change gleaned from various trouser pockets.

It's extremely dark in the countryside, they whimpered over the length of telephone cable; there are no streetlights and last night there was no moon either. "Scared? Who us?" accompanied by derisory but nervous laughter. They slept with torches on, waiting for a trip rope hung with empty tin cans to rattle in the night.

They heard strange, heavy breathing in the small hours and peered cautiously out of the tent flap expecting to see a Welshman pursuing his lady. It turned out to be hedgehogs mating and they told me, with the utmost glee, that they sounded just like human beings. I didn't ask them how they knew that; it seemed to be the highlight of their trip.

Their camping excursion was okay, they told me on their return, loath to admit that my warnings may have been even half right, but next time they thought they might consider bed and breakfast as an option.

How many do you know?

Over the past couple of decades I have been fortunate enough to be on the receiving end of the friendly acquaintanceship of many, and close alliance of a few, carp anglers. Without exception, they are all very macho. They boast about carting mountains of gear across fields, sticking it out in terrible conditions, flood, frost, and famine, for days at a time while they wait for an elusive quarry to take their bait.

Masculinity reigns supreme. They laugh in the face of adversity, wear the same underpants for days at a time, and it seems that the more discomfort they endure in the name of their sport, the more of a man they consider themselves to be. These are the kind of men who wouldn't be seen dead in a pink shirt and as for offering them a slice of quiche you might as well save yourself the trouble.

It was with some surprise, therefore, when a friend told me about his negative experience with a landing net. He had disentangled it from surrounding shrubbery and observed within its folds an assortment of wild flowers. He prides himself on his knowledge of all things fauna, and a fair bit of flora, but was disturbed to discover that there were blossoms among his impromptu bouquet that he could recognise but not put a name to. He seemed quite distraught.

Five quid was all it cost to put him out of his misery. In a local bookshop, I found a Collins Little Gem volume on British wild flowers, bought it, and sent it to him. He was ecstatic, worryingly so, and thanked me profusely. He reckoned that this small and insignificant addition to his library has enhanced his fishing trips immensely. His feminine side seems dangerously near the surface and I just hope for his sake that his mates don't catch on.

Seriously, though, the surroundings in which carp anglers spend best part of their leisure time are not just for reading angling publications, sleeping, eating, and throwing things into water. There is so much going on, if you take the trouble to look, and the wild flower syndrome is just another aspect of enjoying to the full what nature provides.

Indispensible, apparently.

Wild plants still have culinary and medicinal uses today. Our ancestors used them copiously because that was all they had, and some of the uses to which they were put makes interesting reading. Most of us are familiar with the stinging nettle/dock leaf palliative, but if you do get blistered and can't find a dock leaf, then apply the white juice from dandelion stalks. Works like a charm, apparently; I had no idea.

The bane of my summer life is mosquito bites. I'm allergic and if not zapped immediately with something chemical, they erupt into itchy and painful, marble-sized lumps. There are times when I'd forgotten the zapping stuff, though, and I would love to have known about mallow. If you chew mallow stalks (not unpleasant - it tastes sweet) until it is soft and warm and then apply to a mosquito bite it stops the itching for a while. You have to keep doing it all day, but that's a small price to pay, for me.

There are remedies attached to many wild flowers and you could take advantage of all of them while living on riverbanks and at lakesides. There are legends about how they got their names and you can even eat some of them. Have a close look at the plants growing in your swim, next time you're fishing, I guarantee that you'll be surprised at the diverse variety growing there. It's not at all 'girly' - and if you don't agree with my view, the Little Gem books fit neatly into a tackle box so no one need know what you're up to.

One last thing: Gipsywort can be used as a remedy for indigestion but it's also a reputed aphrodisiac. Aha! Got your attention, now, haven't I? I bet Gipsywort will become as rare as rocking-horse droppings beside our waterways as anglers hunt it down and munch it into extinction.

CHAPTER EIGHT

AUGUST OCCASIONS

Thievin' anglers

I always had the most dreadful time keeping hold of freshly cooked food as it cooled off in readiness for the freezer. My family and their friends had squirrel tendencies and when I was in cooking mode they seemed to develop a compulsion to walk in and out of the kitchen, filching the odd morsel on the way in and another on the way out. Trouble was, these morsels added up and there were times when I'd wonder what I'd been doing all day when there was so little to show for my efforts.

Bite-sized items are the most convenient for thieving anglers, of course, and to be fair, it was probably my own fault that I ended up making twice as many sausage rolls, meat patties, muffins than strictly necessary, just to accommodate my apparently starving and transient visitors. I should have gone for the larger baked item. They may have thought twice about stealing a family-sized steak and kidney pie.

"These are nice," said number one son on one of his scrumping forays. He'd come home for the weekend and was taking full advantage. "What's in 'em?"

Elbow deep in a mixing bowl, I was manufacturing fish cakes at a rate of knots. The conveyor belt system was working pretty well but I was at a funny age, still am, come to that; any kind of interruption and I was flummoxed. The concentration went and I was no use to man or beast until I'd had a strong coffee and a lie down. 'What's in 'em?' he wanted to know. Who could say? By the time I had reached the frying/cooling off stage, I'd forgotten the construction details completely.

"I can't remember," I told him. "Prob'ly what I found lurking in the fridge when I started." I began to reel off a list of possible ingredients to nodding approval, until I reached the main component – bass.

His eyebrows rose dramatically and a number of expressions flashed across his face. He was incredulous, disapproving and betrayed. Then I received one of his injured looks.

"We're spoiling you," he said, sadly. "I never thought you would use bass for fish-cakes!" as if I'd committed one of the seven deadly sins or broken a commandment.

What was his problem, for goodness sake? I hadn't *stolen* the bass. I was not the one who had murdered it. There was no adultery involved, sadly, in its procurement and they were not my neighbour's coveted fillets.

"Do they taste okay?" I asked him as he tasted yet another one. They were 'wicked' apparently, but I found myself apologising for using a small sea bass in such an unworthy manner and promised that, next time, I'd stick to whiting or cod. I was made to feel unreasonably guilty and it was only a baby bass, after all. Well, not a baby one, obviously, that would have been illegal, but you know what I mean.

"You'd better give me the recipe, anyway," he said. You wouldn't believe it, would you? Having suitably chastised his mother, he had the barefaced cheek to suggest that he might have a go at bass cakes, himself! Double standards, boy!

Anyway, this is what I told him, in case you fancy having a go:

First, catch a small but legal bass, or steal one from your mother's freezer.

Wrap it very tightly in foil and shove it into an oven that has been pre-heated to medium; that's about 180° C. Leave it alone for 20 minutes, then take it out and leave it to cool off while you make up a couple of rigs, phone your girlfriend, or go for a beer.

As you pull back the foil all the scales, skin and outside bones should come off with it. If they don't, help it along with a knife. Remove the meat from the top half of the fish, strip out the backbone, and remove the rest of the meat. Bundle it all into a large bowl and add a cooked, finely chopped onion and one squashed clove of garlic (or about an inch if you're still using that stuff from a tube). Add a couple of tablespoons (that's the very big one, lovely boy, not the one you eat your breakfast cereal with) of mashed potato plus a few leftover, cooked vegetables that you probably have festering in the bowels of your fridge; sweetcorn and peas are good.

Sling in a handful of porridge oats, two eggs, salt, pepper, and a good pinch of fresh thyme. Hands in and mix thoroughly (remember Play-Doh?) Shape into cakes and fry in hot oil for a couple of minutes each side until they're brown. No flour or breadcrumb coating, please. These are designer fish cakes not tuppence-a-ton, freezer shop specials.

If you can control your impulse to 'taste' them before they cool off, you can freeze them for when you can't be bothered to cook in the evenings. Serve with creamed spuds, sliced green beans and a sauce made like this:

Buy a white sauce mix, follow the instructions on the packet and then add a teaspoonful of horseradish from a jar, salt and pepper. Taste it before you drizzle it all over the bass cakes and adjust seasoning.

I never did find out if number one son ever made bass cakes. Why would he? He just had to turn up in my kitchen and steal the ones I'd made.

Amaized!

I never expected presents from my family when they were on holiday, particularly from abroad. They are always too busy at a water's edge to waste valuable fishing time strolling round towns or villages looking for suitable gifts to take home. I didn't blame them for that. A holiday is supposed to be a time to relax, and wandering around shops, under any circumstances, is my idea of hell on earth. As previosly stated, I hate shopping with a passion.

A few years ago, though, when number one son returned home with half a dozen mates from a carp trip in deepest France, I thought he had changed the habit of a lifetime. A large cool-box, which had been carried in by two of his friends and dumped in front of the freezer door, felt extremely heavy as I tried to move it. Why is it that they always come home starving?

Having convinced myself that the box was full of French wine, cheese...it could be chocolate, perfume...I cooked enough food to feed a small principality, and served it with a smile in anticipation of the revelations that were to follow. I would try to look surprised when presented with gifts from afar.

It was maize. Twenty kilos of maize filled the box to the brim. They had bought it in France because it was cheap and efficient, found they couldn't possibly use all of it in a week and so transported it home for future forays into the English countryside. Fortunately, they'd opted for a 'drive and survive' experience rather than risk an excess baggage fee by plane.

Twenty kilos of maize and two suitcases containing every item of clothing he possessed, covered in French filth and goodness knows what else, were my homecoming gifts. Oh, and half a packet of French mint sweets. They had been so hungry on the journey home, they told me, that they'd been forced to break into my mints but 'half a packet is better than nothing.' No it isn't!

Cool!

There's more about that cool box. It was massive. It had thick rope handles and stood three feet long by eighteen inches wide - don't ask me to give you metric measurements, I still think in 'old money'. It contained a two-feet square freezing compartment which, when fully primed and ready for action, would take about half a ton of crushed ice that weighed...er..about half a ton. Combined with the weight of cans of drink, assorted food, and bait, it became so heavy that it was impossible to lift when loaded.

Once stowed, and accompanied by the Shakespeare box full of more weights and assorted tackle, reels, and so on, a large rod bag containing a variety of rods, just in case, and the brolly, the back of my car was so close to the ground that I held my breath every time I drove over a bump in the road.

Before one summer carp trip, I suggested that we left the cool box at home.

"It's far too heavy,' I said, 'and it's only for your bait really. You could put that into a plastic cool bag, we can put your beer into the lake to keep cool and lukewarm sandwiches won't kill us."

The very idea was dismissed with a gasp of horror.

"We can carry it between us!" said the Chief Angler, determinedly. I could hardly lift my end.

"Why don't we ever use the tackle trolley?" I asked the mandatory stupid question.

"Too noisy," he said, meaning 'too much trouble to retrieve from the garden shed, load and unload'.

He didn't know the meaning of the word. I could show him noisy; piercing screams as my arms dropped off, and why is it that they can never settle for the first available swim? There were no fish in sight, but we still had to walk miles until he was satisfied that his chosen spot was the right one, and that cool box was no lighter on the way back.

Fleas

I had fleas. I seemed to get bitten every time I used my car, but didn't cotton on for a few days. I thought they were mosquito bites until they only developed into lumps the size of a five-pence piece. Mosquitoes leave me with lumps the size of marbles; it seems I'm allergic. I told the Chief Angler about it.

"We must have picked them up from the lake," I said. "Nonsense," he insisted. "It's probably because you haven't cleaned the car out for ages. They're living in the empty crisp packets and Coke tins that the boys leave on the back seat."

He wouldn't have it that the infestation could have anything to do with angling. A bit like when he gets severe indigestion. It's always the fault of a casserole and steamed vegetables, never the large vodka and lemonades he consumed on the way to the dining table.

So, I paid a hasty visit to the local pet shop.

"Can't understand it," I said. "We don't have any pets." The proprietor asked me if my family went camping at all. I told him that they did, kind of, and he informed me that it was easy to transport fleas indoors, which had been living on badgers or foxes.

"You only have to put your rucksack down on a place where an animal has recently lain," he said, "and you only need a couple of fleas to be investigating a rucksack when you place it in a car."

They are capable of breeding prolifically without the least encouragement, apparently, no foreplay and no sense of responsibility toward their offspring. Before you know where you are, you're overrun by the darned things.

I'd only just learned how to keep soft-backed crabs, maggots, and boilies under control, now there were fleas to contend with. Mind you, they were relatively easy to get rid of. I just zapped the car interior with some stuff purchased from the pet shop and after 24 hours, they were ex-fleas. Thank goodness, they hadn't infiltrated the house. I could imagine the grief I'd get. 'Don't touch that! Just because my clothes are in a heap on the floor, doesn't mean they're not clean! That rucksack's packed and ready to go, what are you doing? Just keep away from things you don't understand!'

Mobile phones

Mobile phones can be a darned nuisance. I came to the conclusion that the advantages they bring, of having immediate contact with the outside world just in case of emergency, are far outweighed by the inconvenience to fishing widows/mums on the receiving end. Nephew Paul was one of the first of our group of youngsters to acquire one of these wonders of modern invention and took it everywhere with him which, I suppose, is the general idea. This was, of course, a few years back, before mobiles were considered ideal christening presents.

The boys had decided to camp for a few days at a lake about ten miles away from home. I helped them pack, certain that I'd get rid of them for a few days and would, at last, find the time to prick out several hundred herb seedlings that were growing too big for their trays. They had been crying out to me for help for ages, but this was the school summer holidays and there always seemed to be something I had to do for somebody else. A few hours without a houseful of anglers would be heaven.

The first day of my 'home alone'was wonderful, apart from one call from Paul's phone to say that the eldest had forgotten his hayfever medication and needed it now, immediately. He had packed everything but the kitchen sink from the tackle/bait aspect but carp angling in particular, as every widow knows, takes precedence over health problems. I've witnessed slipped discs and plastered arms at the water's edge; acute migraine or chronic back pain, nothing seems to daunt a determined angler.

I know of those who, having broken a limb, have carried on regardless, played, and landed a carp while in absolute agony from their injury. Only when their prize was safely on the bank did they phone a friend and/or the emergency services. That's not just the one angler, you notice, there have been several over the years, including one who went to sea with a plastered, broken arm and caught the biggest cod on the boat. He had help, I grant you, but not much. In my opinion, he certainly needed help, of the professional variety.

Anyway, back to the phone call from the eldest. If you know that you are acutely allergic to pollen, prolonged exposure to which is likely to bring on an asthma attack and the use of a hospital bed complete with oxygen cylinders and armfuls of aminophylline, it's not entirely sensible to camp out amid long, seeding grass without your medication. How he managed to get a grammar school place used to baffled me at times.

On the evening of the second day, there was a call to say that they'd run out of bread. They hadn't eaten it all; half of it had been thrown in the lake to tempt small, inexperienced roach and bemused bream.

Apparently, they'd read an article in one of the coarse fishing magazines that they had taken along for a bit of light reading and had been experimenting with bread flake. A 20-mile round trip with a couple of medium sliced seemed to do the trick. They were quite happy to promise that the bread would be used for bacon sandwiches; the fish had refused to take part in the experiment, apparently.

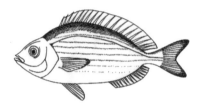

Early the following morning, there was a call to ask for an urgent, and I'd go so far as to say desperate, lift home, on a rota system, mind you. They couldn't leave the rods reeled in but unmanned, despite the presence of friendly bailiffs who were prepared to keep an eye out. They all wanted a poo and told me that the desire to visit a civilised bathroom was due to consideration for other anglers, and the owner of the complex. I pretended to be impressed by their social awareness and agreed to ferry them, one at a time, from the lake to my just-cleaned-to-within-an-inch-of-its-life toilet, but held a sneaking suspicion that their thoughtfulness had more to do with personal comfort.

This was confirmed when the eldest, when it was his turn, partook of a fried breakfast and a bath before requesting the taxi back to base.

After four return trips, I was too exhausted to prick out the seedlings and besides, I had to clean the bathroom again, wash dishes, go shopping to replenish my recently raided cupboards and wash a load of towels.

So, I reckon under-16s with mobile phones should be banned from within five miles of any stretch of water; and have you noticed how the phones have a parent filter? They are never switched on when you need to phone them in an emergency.

Anal-retentive

I showed a list of my 150-odd CDs to a fishing mate. "Blimey, that's a bit anal, isn't it?" he said, astounded because they were in alphabetical order. I tried to defend my penchant for orderliness - only on paper, though, you should see my cupboards - explaining that with so many CDs, tapes and vinyl, the only way to keep track of them (no pun intended) was to catalogue the darned things and keep them stored as per the list.

He and his mates took the pee something chronic until I had to go to one of their bivvies to get some cooking implements.
"The cooker," said Tony, "is on your left as you enter the bivvy. Just under the table and two and a quarter

A shrine to neatness.

inches to the left of the throwing stick."

Okay, I'm exaggerating slightly, but not much. That home from home was absolutely pristine.

There was not a trace of mud on the groundsheet. Everything had been stashed with the aid of a setsquare. Not a speck of dust, a blade of grass or a dead leaf spoiled the symmetry; there was nothing out of place. Made me feel really uncomfortable and as a result, clumsy. I knocked the throwing stick as I went for the cooker, in its own little pouch, drawstring tied in a perfect bow, and worried in case I had replaced it a 'thou' out. He would notice! I kid you not; and he had the nerve to call my CD list anal-retentive!

I strolled thoughtfully back to the 'social' swim where I was to cook their dinner. "Found it, Tone," I said casually. "Couldn't find the tongs though."

He was incredulous.

"You didn't look properly, then," he said. "I know exactly where everything is in that bivvy." The man is proud of the fact that his tent is a shrine to orderliness and woe betides anyone who hints that there is a flaw in his system.

"I didn't like to poke about," I said defensively. "Everything is so...shiny."
He retrieved the cooking tongs himself and, to my relief, didn't comment on the position of the throwing stick.

An after-dinner, and several glasses of something, discussion revealed that his own home is not as tidy as his lakeside retreat, but this made it all the more fascinating as we watched him polish a no longer required bank-stick to perfection. Fishing, I deduced, is similar to religion and we had among us a disciple of such fervour that he treated his living quarters as a temple.

His tackle box, being the altar from which all good catches originate, is an example of extreme obsession. Everything is filed in its proper place and he has

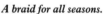

A braid for all seasons.

everything labelled. He even has a row of PVA string, meticulously graded in sequence - left to right - from summer to winter, rain through to 80-degree heat, interspersed by 'turned out nice again', 'pleasant for the time of year,' 'a bit dodgy over Will's Mum's' and finally, 'if all else fails, I'll use this.' If an item of tackle is removed from the tackle box, it is used, then immediately polished into gleaming cleanliness, and replaced in exactly the same position from which it was taken.

Don't get me wrong, I've just read this through and it sounds as if I'm criticising the man for his organisation skills. I'm not, I promise you. He's a lovely bloke and I admire his methodical approach. I just don't think he has the right to call me anal-retentive when he is clearly withholding far more. At least I don't have a re–tent–ive bivvy. (Geddit?)

The other extreme.

Moreover, despite any rumours you may hear to the contrary, I am not at all envious of his state-of-the-art, portable DVD player with 5" screen and mini-surround sound. Much. Hardly at all jealous. If he wants to watch 'Dances With Carp' while waiting for a screaming run, that's up to him. I'm quite happy with my charity shop paperback. I will just mention that this fairly decent bit of kit is constructed almost entirely of lustrous stainless steel and there is not a finger-mark to be seen upon it! It lives, a quarter inch to the right of a transistor radio, facing south-east in a perfectly tensioned bivvy. We swear he's into feng shui.

By comparison, the 'social' bivvy, around which we all gather at every mealtime, is a complete tip - like my cupboards and drawers - and yet the man who owns it is just as fervent about his fishing and catches just as often as his tackle-tart friend. He feels more comfortable and relaxed if he doesn't have to be forever tidying up, he says. Each to their own.

Catch of a lifetime

I can't believe I did it. After 20-odd years of sitting and watching other people dangling things in water and professing to have a good time, I finally caught a fish of my very own. We had been invited to a quiet, private, Hampshire lake for a fun day out. I took, as usual, enough food to feed anyone who happened by and prepared to do what I do best, i.e. dispensing food, comforting words and encouragement, if needed, never dreaming that I would end up experiencing such a moving encounter with something scaly.

We arrived early morning, just as a mist was lifting off the water, and disturbed dozens of feeding rabbits, watching their white tails bob to safety into the woods as we followed tyre tracks in the dew toward a huge oak tree where we were to be based for the day. A swamp cypress, which I was told becomes tinged with copper in winter, stood proud in a reed bed while a woodpecker stuck itself vertically to the side of a beech.

Cows were lowing in adjacent fields, wood pigeons cooed, baby robins squeaked and the lake was flat calm. Absolute heaven.

The CA set up all his gear while I unpacked the food baskets and placed a huge cool box under a tree so that people could help themselves to a cold drink or a sandwich if they happened to be passing. I was perfectly happy and drifted into 'thinking and observation' mode.

Concentrating – don't speak to me.

Time seemed to fly by. Lunchtime came and went before we knew it. There were still sounds of birdsong in early afternoon and droning bumblebees cruised by, buzzed by brilliantly hued dragonflies. A grass snake swam lazily sideways causing convoluted eddies to break on the surface of the water and I could hear gentle movement in the surrounding vegetation from small creatures going about their business. Despite the arrival of several families accompanied by small, excited children carrying inflated armbands and beach balls (there's a separate swimming pool set back from the lake, they were not about to jump all over the carp) the ambience was still tranquil and almost sleep-inducing.

Far from being slightly bored, as I had expected to be, words began to fill my head and when that happens there is no going back, I have to write them down or they just continue to go round and round, like one of those ticker-tape machines they used to have in Piccadilly Circus. Inspiration having struck, I was spread-eagled on a blanket, writing a few notes when our host called to me. 'Ere, Rose,' he said, 'come and hold this.'

I looked up immediately, ever willing to be helpful and thinking that maybe he wanted an extra hand for something or other piscatorial. No such thing. He handed me a whip, fully-loaded with maggot and showed me how to pop it into the water; he even told me when to pull it out. 'Now! Now, Rosie! Strike and lift,' and there it was; my first ever fish, a baby crucian carp. It was only about four inches long but the excitement it engendered was beyond my imagination. I had no idea that everything trembles when you catch something, me included. No one previously had bothered to explain about that magical sensation from a hooked fish that goes up the line, through the rod and into the body. Until it happened to me, I hadn't been able to understand why anglers become so obsessed. Now, I was beginning to.

"Wow!" I exclaimed and turned to the CA. "Why have you never allowed me to do this before?"

There was no reply but his face was a picture. For some reason, he wasn't over the moon about my discovery or enthusiasm. I never got to the bottom of it, either. I still don't know why.

"If you want to do it again," said my instructor, "you'll have to learn how to put a maggot on and take the hook out all by yourself." Never in a million years would I have dreamt of such a thing before that crucian, but I'd fallen in love with it and wanted another one. Such was my exhilaration that I fought back my usual repulsion toward wriggling things and, gritting my teeth, put the hook through a maggot. This went on for several hours and I caught loads. The worst bit was trying to remove the hook. I was so scared that I was going to hurt my little friends, and it would be some time before I had the courage to master a disgorger, but I found that, nine times out of ten, I only had to wiggle it a bit and the hook fell free.

This is fun!

The proper anglers, of course were catching real carp but I was perfectly happy getting crucians, a bite a chuck; until I got home, that is, when I began to wonder what it feels like to catch a really big mirror or common. I vowed to be forever grateful to my friend who was thoughtful enough to introduce me to the joys of fishing and one day, I determined, I would catch a proper carp.

CHAPTER NINE

SEPTEMBER IN THE RAIN

Rain of terror

Recently, I spent a day sitting under a bivvy in persistent, heavy rain, with nothing to do but think. This is absolute bliss, for me. I'm always busy, rushing around after others mostly, and rarely have time to sit and stare. As a child, I lived in a 'prefab.' with a flat roof and so the sound of raindrops on taut canvas brings back memories of childhood. I find it very comforting; a box of Smarties, a copy of Enid Blyton's Sunny Stories and I'd have been in heaven. I allowed my mind to travel backwards.

During his 'unemployed and don't know what I want out of life' phase, the eldest went to East Germany, at short notice, to look for work with a couple of mates. Finding employment wasn't a problem. The place was almost derelict and so underdeveloped that they were crying out for workers in the construction industry. They must have been! Number one son's last job in the UK had been as a darkroom technician with journalistic tendencies and he got a job in Leipzig as a ceiling fixer. Trying to get hard-earned cash for several weeks' work out of the Germans, however, proved to be a different matter so he gave up after a month or two and came home, completely skint and still owed several weeks' wages. He never did get paid.

I picked him up at Heathrow. He was depressed, broke and without hope. He'd really missed his fishing, he said. There was no time for the love of his life in Germany. They had been working 12-hour days, six days a week; Sundays he spent sleeping. He had missed the start of the season for the first time ever, so he was only home a matter of hours before organising a long-anticipated carping expedition for the following day. His brand new bivvy, bought with the last of his redundancy money, two days before the German adventure took off, was erected in the garden to make sure all was as it should be. I 'loaned' him a tenner so that he

Thinking in the rain.

could purchase a set of bivvy pegs with which to secure it to the ground and he was raring to go.

A batch of fresh boilies was hurriedly manufactured to top up the supply that had been made and frozen a couple of months previously, and plenty of sandwiches were made to accompany the mountain of chocolate bars and crisps that are apparently a vital ingredient to lakeside well-being if you're under 25. Eggs, bacon, burgers and sausages were bought and stored in a cool box for the early morning fry-up and he was ready to go.

In England, there had been no rain for several weeks and it was a glorious September day when the eldest and a fishing mate set out in anticipation of 24-hours or so of blissful lakeside activity. An hour later, they arrived at their chosen venue; it was an unfamiliar lake because since the East German trip they'd developed the taste for adventure and the unknown. It was raining quite heavily but they weren't worried. The brand new bivvies took only minutes to put up in the one available swim, while rucksacks waited patiently in the downpour where they had been dumped, unceremoniously and without a thought for the consequences, for their quarters to be prepared. Rod bags had been left in the car until camp had been properly set up.

Once set up, they placed all the equipment inside the bivvies and began the task of preparing bedchairs to receive bodies that they hoped would soon be exhausted through reeling in 30-pounders. On opening their rucksacks, the boys discovered that rainwater had seeped through, saturating pillows and the spare clothing they had taken along 'just in case we have a shower and get slightly damp.' They would have been better off wearing a pair of swimming trunks and anticipating wearing the spare clothes 'just in case it stops.'

The rain, which had been forecast as 'occasional showers' continued for 15 hours solid, interspersed with thunder, lightning and squally gusts of wind, all of which did nothing for the watertight qualities of their bivvies. After a couple of hours of serious precipitation, odd drips began to seep through the heat-sealed seams. Gradually, these drips spread over a larger area until the roof of one bivvy was leaking like a sieve and the other dripped rainwater with quite an interesting rhythm into a strategically placed saucepan on the bivvy floor.

The lads had put the rod bags underneath the bed-chairs, after removing the contents and setting up by the water's edge, so only the unimportant items, such as sleeping bags, food and clothing received a soaking. By dusk, they were wet through but determined not to give in to the elements. They were convinced that the carp might yet begin to feed as the temperature had dropped considerably compared to the recent hot weather, although it was still quite warm.

They decided that it was time to light the Coleman stove and placed it, just inside the open front of number one son's bivvy. His shelter wasn't leaking as badly as his companion's tent so the Coleman had at least a fighting chance of staying lit. They started a mammoth fry-up for comfort. If they fried everything at once and at a high enough heat, they reasoned, maybe the fat fumes from bacon, sausages and burgers would create a seal on the bivvy roof.

The cooking stint was carried out by the First Mate who, unthinkingly, placed a red-hot frying pan on the plastic groundsheet before transferring the kettle to the hob to boil for tea. So, not only was the bivvy leaking from above, but there was a large hole in the groundsheet, and still they refused to admit defeat and return home. They sat there all night in the pouring rain, inside the bivvies with sleeping bags over their heads to keep off the worst of the weather and waited in vain for any sign of action from the lake.

"D'you think they field-tested these bivvies?' asked the First Mate. "Oh, yes," replied the eldest. "I'm sure they did, but not in Burma during the monsoon season, which is what it's getting like out there. Don't panic! It's bound to stop soon."

It didn't. They hadn't had so much as a nibble, at least from the fish. They, on the other hand, had eaten everything that wasn't completely sodden, were in possession of two, almost brand new but ailing bivvies, one with a ventilation hole in the floor and another which would have to be sprayed with vulcanised rubber solution and pebble-dashed before it could be used in a light shower. At last, they decided that enough was enough.

Why does it take so long for it to sink in? The boys were not alone in their determination to sit it out under any conditions. I know of other carp anglers who seem to think they are on a mission with the SAS, or halfway up Annapurna, when to break camp would be a major undertaking. All any of them have to do is to chuck everything in the back seat, jump into a car and drive toward sanctuary. Hot baths, warm food, and dry clothes are never more than a few miles away. Maybe it's a man thing and they think it's girly to give in; I don't know.

Anyway, back to the plot. The boys evicted rucksacks into the rain, along with rod-bags, while the bivvies were dismantled and thrust into their little hold-alls, which took a maximum of ten minutes. Wonderful inventions, bivvies, it certainly beats wrestling with a dome tent in a force eight, as I've been known to do when my boys were small and demanded to be taken fishing in the school holidays.

They arrived home very wet, hungry, tired, and dispirited, to sort out their gear on the hall carpet, which began to think seriously about mildew.
"You should tell the manufacturers about the bivvies, boys," I told them. "Far better to let them know than to slag them off. At least give them a chance to defend themselves."

Number one son decided that he couldn't justifiably complain since his bivvy wasn't leaking too badly, taking into consideration the dire weather conditions, and it was his mate who had created the ventilation shaft in the floor; few companies guarantee against allowing divvies into bivvies. The eldest assured me that he would wear a sou'wester and oilskins when he next used it in heavy rain.

His friend, though, duly carted his bivvy, along with every piece of fishing luggage he possessed, to the shop where he'd bought it and explained his predicament, whereupon he was promised a swiftish repair job and the loan of another bivvy while he was waiting. No one, he was told, guarantees copiously zipped luggage as 100% waterproof. Showerproof, maybe, but not torrential, cat and dog-proof; not in rain so heavy that 19 London underground stations were closed the next day due to flooding.

To their credit, when the manufacturers heard that the First Mate's mate's bivvy had also sprung a leak, they insisted on being given the chance to repair that, too. We had no rain for weeks after that!

A Carp of my own

I offer no apology for boasting about my very first weighable fish. It was a tench, weighed about five pounds and the CA let me catch it on a match rod while he was carp fishing one Sunday. I really wanted a carp and during that particular summer, my goal was to catch a decent-sized one. I was determined to do it. In fact, I nearly did it just after I'd caught the tench and if it hadn't been for some unwarranted interference, I might have realised my dream.

I had bought myself a rod licence so that I could fish legally, but the difficult bit was persuading the CA that I was serious. I'd gone up to our local club water after work, where he had been since I'd dropped him off at daybreak and I was more than ready for my first proper carp lesson.

"Oh, good!" he said, as I dumped a picnic hamper containing home-cooked goodies and what felt like a ton of liquid refreshment on the bank beside him. I'd just lugged it all for several hundred yards through briar and bramble but was he grateful for meals on wheels? Was he heck as like.
"I'm glad you've turned up," he said, ignoring my carefully prepared comestibles. "Now I can get me other two rods out." The rods I was supposed to be using, please note.

Could he not spare the time for a roast beef sarnie or a cup of lovingly percolated and freshly vacuumed coffee? Not likely, there were far more important issues to address. There was no time to waste on mundane pastimes like eating and drinking. He handed me a match rod with which I could amuse myself while he concentrated on more serious business and proceeded to prepare 'my' carp rods with indecent haste, before finally collapsing, breathless and exhausted on to his chair.

Ten minutes later, a buzzer sounded, and you can guess whose rod was responding. Unfortunately, I had been placed (by Himself) furthest away from the carp rods and with a large tackle box and the food between us. I realised later that this was a deliberate move so that he would have easy access

Me and my tench.

to any action, although he swore that this was just the way it worked out. No malice aforethought whatsoever, he said.

As the CA picked up the active rod, I could see by the curve in it that there was a decent fish on and knew that it had to be a carp. I stood up, navigated my way past the obstacles, and anticipated the hand over, but

I should have known what would happen.

"I'll just get it away from the reeds for you," he said, which was very considerate of him, obviously. "It just needs to be coaxed into clear water. You'll never manage to get it over those snags. I'll just get it a bit nearer. Bit more. Get the net! Get the net!"

No wonder, he looked smug in the photo. That should have been my carp, my very first.
"You'd only have lost it," he said, when I at first remonstrated then sulked and ate all the not-squashed sandwiches before he could get to them, out of spite. He was probably right but I would have liked to know what it felt like to lose a fine carp.

I was telling an angling friend about this incident, expecting sympathy and righteous indignation on my behalf about the injustice of it all but he interrupted my diatribe on the selfishness of some grown-up anglers not a million miles away.
"Oh, come on, Rosie," he said. "That's perfectly normal behaviour. I wouldn't have given you the rod, either. You would have lost the fish and that's just not an option if it can be avoided. Lighten up!"

Well, I didn't 'lighten up'. I'd set my heart on that carp. I was very disappointed and remained so until I had redressed the balance, and I bet you're thinking 'childish and pathetic'. I already know that. The knowledge doesn't help!
Bitter? Me? Too right! I got one eventually, though, thanks to a little help from my friends.

Spiderman

The Chief Angler is an arachnophile. We had only been married a few weeks when I found out that he had a thing about spiders; he considered them to be special and his personal friends. In the days when I vacuumed carpets whether they needed cleaning or not, before I realised that life is too short to perform unnecessary acts of housework, I was hoovering the bedroom floor when a large spider foolishly decided to go for a walk. I didn't stand a chance; it ran straight out in front of me, officer, and I ran over him with my appliance.

The CA was distraught. He didn't swear and shout or admonish me in any way for murdering his little acquaintance but he was deeply moved.
"Oh, no!" he said sadly. "He's been living in my sock drawer for ages."
I took care, during the following 20-odd years, never to repeat my crime and resigned myself to the fact that we'd always have lodgers.

He had spent all of one wet and windy Sunday morning constructing a drop net in readiness for an anticipated late-summer sea fishing trip. Well made, weighted, sturdy enough to stand up to all manner of weather conditions, this net was placed in a black sack and stored in the garden shed until required.

Come the day, he was off with the usual complement of friends, on a smoothhound hunt. He nearly left home without the drop net, his memory being similar to my own, but remembered at the last minute, grabbed the net from the shed and toddled off seawards.

It was a late tide so the lads met early and enjoyed a slap-up breakfast at the wharfside café and discussed their strategy for the day. They were looking forward, they said, to using the new-ish piece of equipment constructed for the common good by the CA and for which he received due praise and universal approval. They intended to trawl with it for hermit crab and shrimp to use as bait, confident that because of the wondrous net they would return victorious on the evening tide having caught and released a multitude of near-record-breaking 'hounds. (smoothhounds or tope, for the uninitiated.)

As soon as they were aboard, the Chief Angler placed the sack containing the net on the deck and was surprised, besides being more than a little touched, to find that Essfer (S for spider) had decided to abandon his family for the day (as had the CA) and had come along for the trip. The CA told me later that he had noticed a couple of dozen babies on a web in the shed near where the net had been stored, so he knew this spider was a parent.

Essfer emerged cautiously from the black sack, stood still and looked around before wandering off for a stroll and a reconnoitre of his surroundings. He was gone for about 20 minutes and then returned to the net for a lie down. The spider repeated his little outings every hour or so, every time returning to the net bag, and remained quite safe because the CA was keeping an eye on him. It's hard to believe that the spider didn't just launch itself into the drink or disappear into the bowels of the cabin, but it's true, so I was told; it kept coming back.

So far, the CA hadn't told his mates about his little friend. He knew that he would have to sooner or later because they might want to use the drop net, and he knew there was no way he could allow that. If the net were removed and soaked in the briny, Essfer would have no secure hiding place.

Inevitably, one of the more observant members of the party spotted the spider-lover's preoccupation with the drop net and the CA was forced to confess, quietly that he was harbouring a stowaway.

"Let's put it in Jim's reel bag for a laugh,' suggested one of the anglers and did just that before the CA could protest. Fortunately, Essfer was too wily to fall for that one and instead of shouting 'Boo!' as Jim picked it up, skilfully abseiled out of the bag and scurried back into his drop net sanctuary.

The anglers did catch despite the distraction so my freezer was nicely stocked with bass and thornback. The smoothies and dogfish they did manage to hook by using previously harvested crab, were released to swim another day but the drop net stayed a virgin and was likely to remain so. Very late that night, it was replaced carefully in the garden shed next to the web of babies who, I dare say, were overjoyed at the return of the prodigal parent.

I always tried my best to understand the way anglers think, I really did and I still do, but it makes no sense when I know for a fact, because I'd seen it happen, that they will put anything that wriggles on a hook in an attempt to lure a fish. I also know that, during the Essfer trip, the CA had torn the legs off crabs, rammed hooks through their still squirming bodies, and forced them to bungee jump into the sea.

Essfer, however, just a few places below his cousins in the food chain, was fêted like royalty, nurtured, and treated with respect. He was even taken to the pub for a couple of hours and an after trip pint, even if he was dumped in a corner of the snug with the rest of the tackle. The only conclusion I can come up with is that the CA might have been a spider in a previous life. He could certainly spin a good yarn.

Tide table

The youngest has always been a coarse angler at heart. A pike/carp devotee, he was never really interested in sea fishing except when tackle was being sorted out by other anglers in the house in preparation for a forthcoming venture on to the high seas. During this ritual, he would hover nearby and scrutinise closely every item, occasionally 'borrowing' the occasional hook or weight from the sea-tackle boxes in case they might come in handy for heavy-duty pike catching.

There came a time though, in a weak moment and under the influence of his newly discovered taste for lager, that he allowed himself to be persuaded to go along with big brother and his motley crew of mates on a beach fishing trip. "Don't panic. We'll take the bivvies, lamps, cookers and stuff," he was reassured by the expert. "You might even get to like it."

There was just one problem. The youngest didn't own a sea rod. Carp/pike rods would not do to cast from the beach and since all the others in the eldest's rod collection couldn't possibly be loaned to a mere brother because they were going to be used by assorted friends, he couldn't go along unless he acquired his own equipment.

He didn't mind; he was quite happy not to bother, but number one son was determined that his little brother would receive his sea baptism and so together they began to beg, borrow and steal. They started by scrounging an old and decrepit sea reel from a friend of their father's. It took two days to take it to bits, lay it all out on the dining room table, oil, rust-remove, and reassemble. They were halfway there but the actual rod was beyond the youngest's pocket, even if he had been prepared to fork out hard-earned cash on something he would probably only use a couple of times.

"There's an old beachcaster in the shed," their father told them from the depths of an armchair. "You can have that, if you like. It'll need a bit of tarting up but it's not a bad rod."

It turned out to be a 12-foot fibreglass blank that a South African friend had left behind when he'd returned to his native land some 15 years previously. It had not seen the light of day since then and was currently being colonised by quite a large spider community who had lived there for several generations, assumed squatters' rights and now considered it to be their family seat.

Despite the CA's love of spiders, guess who had to brave the arachnid clan and demand the rod's return into polite society. The spiders were a tad miffed when I approached them politely and suggested that they relinquish their present property and move house to a more permanent site. After wrestling with the patriarch of the colony for a minute or so, though, he gave up and scuttled off in a huff while my junior anglers and their mates all watched from a safe distance. How can nearly grown men, who have caught and battled with conger eels, be afraid of spiders? It beats me.

Many times over the next few days, I wished that I had left the rod to its fate. The dining room table was commandeered, yet again, by the youngest while the blank was held securely in a padded vice and sanded down; the wet 'n' dry emery paper necessary for the task having been bought by me in the interests of a quiet life.

Afraid of spiders? Me?

It was considered by all to be a household commodity and should not, therefore, have to be bought with fag and beer money. I was out-voted, as usual. Sometimes it was hard being the only female in the gang.

They slapped on one coat of varnish and I thought I might be able to have my table back, but apparently not.

Three times this sanding/varnish operation had to be performed; essential, they said, so that salt water couldn't penetrate. Three days on and it was finally finished. Now I could eat like a civilised human being instead of trying to cut up my dinner on a tray balanced precariously on my lap. Wrong again.

Rod rings had to be meticulously whipped into place and I was told that it would be much easier to deal with if the blank was kept in the vice while this precision work was undertaken. Of course it would, silly me. Why did I not anticipate the obvious? Then the finished rings had to be varnished, twice. At last, the tip was painted a garish, luminous yellow and the whole thing proudly displayed to the world. It only took me a couple of hours to clean up the table and the surrounding floor space. I made myself some tea and toast and sat at the table to eat it. It was like welcoming back an old friend.

The day dawned and they were off for a day's sport, after raiding the larder and taking with them enough food to feed a regiment. The youngest caught a small flounder on the new rod, more by luck than good judgement, I fear, and then returned home, put the rod back in the shed and allowed the spiders to move back into their old home. He never used the rod again and it was to be a decade, or more, before he ventured on to the high seas again with his brother. All that unnecessary suffering and inconvenience to spiders and a fishing mother. What was the point?

Land ho! Mr Christian!

"When was the last time you rowed a boat, Rose?" The question was asked early morning after an over-nighter with some friends.

"I don't think I ever have," I said. "My Dad used to row me around the boating pool in Southend when I was a kid. There used to be a geezer with a megaphone who shouted 'Come in number 2, your time is up,' after the paid for half an hour was spent, but I haven't ever rowed myself."

There was no response to this dip into nostalgia. My interrogator was rootling about in a rucksack. I assumed he hadn't heard me and continued studying the lake.

"Put this on," said a voice, and I turned to walk into a life jacket held up by the question master. "It's beautiful out there on the lake," he said, enthusiastically. "If we (note the 'we') can get to the island you can see where the swans live and it's very peaceful over there; totally unspoiled."

He held me and the boat steady as he urged me to descend the bank and to step into what can only be described as a large fibreglass box with a point on one end. I had assumed that he was going to follow me into the boat. Stupid woman! Can't think why that crossed my mind. I really should have known better since there was only the one milk crate to sit upon and water was swishing around in the bottom of the boat. Although my companions were close friends, and still are, surprisingly, they're not that close that they'll sit

I'm not coming back!

in a couple of inches of stagnant water in the bottom of a boat for me!

I sat facing the island and waited for the anticipated extra weight to climb in behind me.
"Pick up that paddle, then. The one down by your side," was the next command.
Conditioned, I dutifully did as I was bid, and turned my head to see a boot on the square bit at the back of the boat, pushing it away from the bank.

Panic? If you want to see panic, you should have been there. I smiled sweetly (must keep up the image - good old Rosie, always game for a laugh) and muttered obscenities under my breath aimed at the male of the species in general, illegitimate sons of female dogs, all of them, even on occasions like these, the ones who purported to be friends.

To be fair, they did stand at the water's edge and, in between giggling manically, offered words of advice. "Maybe you'd better do two strokes each side, Rose, since you've been paddling for ten minutes and haven't moved." This yelled at me when I was in the middle of the lake and had hit some kind of current that, no matter how hard I paddled, pushed me back to where I had started - apparently. I had no idea this was happening. I'd thought I was doing all right until yelled at.

Once I'd got the hang of it, though, it became an adventure. Swallows and Amazons had been one of my favourite books as a child. I was exploring alone in uncharted territory, a single paddle and an upturned milk crate my only tools. Who knew what strange and wonderful life forms I could encounter!

Meanwhile, the strange and wonderful life forms on the opposite bank were, they told me later, becoming a tad worried. I had been gone quite some time and although one of them is a qualified lifesaver, the distance I had covered was enough to have me drown before he could get to me. That's if he could find me in the first place for I had found a narrow opening and ventured through it. It was like entering into a fantasy world. It was so quiet, apart from scurrying wildlife that carried on as usual, undisturbed by my small craft cruising through their domain. The light changed to a kind of mysterious green with shafts of refracted sunlight flashing through as the trees above obligingly moved their branches to admit it. I could imagine myself alone on the earth. Given a large

Cadbury and a bottle of water I could easily have stayed there all day.

All traces of resentment for my cruel treatment had vanished by the time I had collected my wits and paddled back from whence I came. My friends had lost interest in my watery expedition and refused to listen to my poetic descriptions of an enchanted environment. They were in preoccupied and slightly depressed, packing up mode and had seen it all before, anyway. I suspect that I had been cast adrift in an open boat, with no provisions, to get me out of the way while this process was executed but I'm grateful. Another 'first time' experience and I loved it.

Now, where did I put…?

Just an observation, here; I noticed, while on a fishing trip with some friends, all of whom are highly intelligent and not the least bit dim, that they seemed to be obsessed with everything camo.

They wear camo clothes, including underpants. I only know about the latter through hearsay, you understand, I don't have any proof - well, hardly any. They take pride in possessing the latest gizmos: camouflaged sunglasses, including the lenses, hats, gloves, luggage, small pouches to put 'things' in - even a camouflaged, collapsible knife and fork set, for goodness sake. Like the carp are really going to watch them eating and, selectively, not notice the three feet wide and totally uncamouflaged barbecue set-up blazing away on the bank.

Where did I put those camouflaged scales?

Yeah, right. The sunglasses will make you invisible!

Why all this need for secrecy and disguise? After a couple of beers, not only can they not see each other but they can't find any of their equipment, either. Everything looks the same, predominantly like leaves and twigs. It's distressing for an onlooker to witness the needless, and often fruitless, hunting through their gear, performed by friends and loved ones as they try to find a camouflaged bait-needle that they had put down just seconds before. It's like watching someone searching for a stick insect in a compost heap.

Why?

The photos I've used to illustrate this obsession for concealment were taken a few years ago but it shows you how the more sinister form of the illness can start. Be warned - before you too succumb to WheretheHelldidIput-itis.

CHAPTER TEN

OCTOBER - STRANGER THINGS HAVE HAPPENED

Pike trace

October is the time for ghosties, ghoulies and things that go 'splash' in the night. It also heralds the start of the pike fishing season proper. Watch your most personal possessions at this time of the year if you live with anglers. Things mysteriously disappear if you are not vigilant and you never see them again.

One dark, October evening, the youngest found his violin buried under a pile of memorabilia in the attic. He hadn't touched it for several years, let alone practised and was as surprised as the rest of his family that he could still remember how to play it.

Caught with the aid of a violin.

We spent a pleasant half an hour in the music room while he ran through all his old exam pieces, with me accompanying on the piano and reminiscing about the fun we used to have when he and his brother were small and musical, as against big and piscatorial.

Then he whipped out the E string and declared that it would make a decent pike trace. "Good idea," said his father, eyeing up my baby grand. "We used to use piano wire, years ago."

Just let 'em try!

Pike au beurre noir

You may be given gifts of love and devotion, whether you like it or not. The real pike season begins on 1st October and shortly after this date, you could discover a squidgy parcel wrapped in layers of plastic bags, lurking nastily on a refrigerator shelf. Do not open it, yet. You will be told what it is and that is enough, believe me. Under no circumstances should you show any enthusiasm.

I had telephone calls, during the morning, from my great white hunters, asking how the culinary preparations were going. I made excuses for as long as I could. The washing, ironing, cleaning, visiting elderly relatives who live in Spain, had to be done first before I could even think about preparing food of any description.

The eldest asked what my problem was. "It's only a pike, for goodness sake," he said. "You eat all the sea fish that I bring home. What's the difference?" I didn't know. It just didn't seem right, somehow. Years of conditioning, I suppose. Maybe if I'd seen pike fillets alongside the smoked haddock and tubs of freshly cooked prawns in our local wet fish shop, I'd have been more inclined to accept it as a food source. Mind you, they did sell carp at Jewish holiday times, but that didn't seem right either.

The youngest told me that I was a bit on the pathetic side and also began the 'it's only a pike, for goodness sake' argument until I cut him short. "You'd never survive living off the land in the countryside," he muttered. I don't have a problem. I have no hankering after that version of the good life. As long as there are nice, full supermarket shelves, butcher, and greengrocer's shops handy, I'm as happy as a pig in muck.

Eventually, I had to get down to it, look for a recipe, shop for the ingredients missing from the store cupboard; white wine, shallots, a leek, fresh parsley, chives and thyme, a bay leaf and then, when I'd gathered everything, it was time to open my present at last. I did it while holding my breath and after the briefest of cursory glances at all those teeth, I hastily covered it up again and took two paracetamol followed by a fun-sized Mars bar.

I let my present soak for a couple of hours in salted water then dried it off, stuffed it with the herbs and vegetables, covered it in white wine, tin-foiled it and shoved the whole mess into the oven for 20 minutes or so. Once cooked, it didn't look too bad, a bit prehistoric, maybe, because I hadn't bothered to remove the head and tail, but accompanied by a pile of mashed potato and some frozen peas, I thought it would pass muster.

When they rushed through the front door, at the appointed time, en route to the kitchen as they always did, they inspected my efforts and said something like, "Er...well, actually...erm, I'm not all that hungry at the moment and, anyway, I'm going out for a curry later."

This was bullshit. They were always and without exception starving after a day at work. I made a fuss, created merry hell and forced them to taste it, at least, before giving the leftovers to the dog. "What's the matter?" I got my own back. "It's only a pike, for goodness sake!"

I had quite a peaceful evening. I knew they'd invent some errand that would take them near to the fast food restaurants. To be fair, before they went they said all the right things in appreciation of my efforts and made loud, enthusiastic, smacking noises with their mouths, but they didn't eat any of it. I was never presented with another pike.

Pansies

Stupidly, I'd planted a load of winter pansies in anticipation of a cheerful display the following season, when they eventually burst into flower. I took so much trouble over those plants, nurtured the little devils for weeks and was really looking forward to sitting at my office window with a cup of tea as they nodded their heads to me in a light, spring breeze.

Oh well, it looked like I was going to be depressed during the cold and dark months, because somebody dug 'em up again, by mistake apparently, in the dark while harvesting earthworms for a bream trip. By the time I found out about it, they had lost most of their leaves and their upturned roots had been seriously disturbed by passing wildlife. They were ex-pansies.

He was very apologetic and did buy me some new ones, but why the eldest hadn't employed his usual pastime of throwing what they called 'Fairy Up Liquid' over the lawn and waiting until the worms came gasping and screaming to the surface, I have no idea. Difficult to spot in the dark, I suppose.

Hoarders

I've come to the conclusion that most anglers have squirrel tendencies. After a fairly lengthy 'preparing to go fishing' session during which I was bombarded by all three anglers in my family with 'I can't find... What have you done with...?' I waved them off and decided to sort out their respective clothes cupboards. An afternoon spent organising while elbow deep in whiffy wardrobes, I reasoned, would be a small price to pay for a trouble-free, getting ready period next time they went.

No wonder they couldn't find anything wearable. Among the debris there were holey jumpers, T-shirts with the sleeves cut out, gloves minus fingers, ancient boots with no laces, perished sou'westers, a kamikaze pilot's hat, which had been home to several generations and species of moth, open-plan wader socks and a number of jackets with broken zips.

I removed everything that I wouldn't be seen dead in and threw it into a heap on the landing, ready for a trip to the local tip; it wasn't fit for any charity shop. This rubbish removal would take place, I decided, after a well-deserved coffee and when I had summoned up the energy to transfer it all into black sacks. My argument when they returned was going to be, 'if you haven't worn/used it for two or more years, then you don't really need it'.

There was *hell* to pay when they came back. I had been sidetracked by several cups of coffee and a visiting friend so the mess was still festering where I had left it. Accompanied by muttered curses, quite a bit of the junk was rescued and lovingly replaced into neat and nearly empty wardrobes. Just how many lucky jumpers could one man possess? I was assured that it would all come in handy for fishing one day, and at the same time was castigated for 'interfering'. "Just leave things alone that you know nothing about," they said. There's gratitude!

Genetic

Recently, I had confirmed to me what I've always suspected, that one of the qualifications required to be a successful carp angler is to be ever-so-slightly mentally unbalanced. Going through my million or so photos while searching for one to illustrate an article, I came across a few that portray this disturbance in all its glory.

I showed them to a couple of fellow fishing widows who happened to be visiting and was surprised to learn that they, too, were in possession of similar photos and occasionally, were given cause for concern about their anglers' state of mind. They had been too embarrassed or ashamed to show these pictures to anyone and had hidden them at the backs of drawers but they were very grateful, they said, that I had come out. Their relief at knowing that they were not the only ones with dodgy family members knew no bounds.

During what seemed like a group therapy session, I was told of a carp angler who makes a habit of driving 50 miles or more in dire weather conditions, just to check out a 'new' lake, not to actually fish it mind, but to assess the size and dietary preferences of the carp within it. He takes careful note of the surrounding trees and assorted shrubbery, chats up resident anglers, then mentally chooses a swim that

This is how it starts.

In the advanced stages. *Beyond hope.*

he fancies fishing after he has had time to calculate the number and flavours of boilies required for a couple of days' fishing, and the type of rig appropriate to the venue.

Once all this had been ascertained, apparently, he revisits the water on alternate days, suffering a 100-mile return trip, and throws bait into the chosen swim; no fishing involved at this stage. This is a common strategy and not at all unusual behaviour, according to the anglers who do it. We thought it was weird. Like window-shopping, in a way; we couldn't see the point of that either.

During the consumption of several cups of coffee, we discussed the angling phenomenon further; I made a large pot in the end, heavy on the caffeine. We speculated on the likely reasons that our menfolk habitually bivvy up beside a lake in fog, snow, hurricane or blinding rain, allow their bodies to get soaking wet, first degree wind-burn or frost-bitten and still profess enjoyment.

Maybe it's to get away from us, we thought, but only briefly. No! It couldn't possibly be that. Clearly, this is an inherited genetic disorder, carried from the male side.

On yer toes

Nothing is sacred. They even pinched my toenail clippers. Apparently, they are ideal for dealing with the wire traces used during pike-hunting trips. On three separate occasions I bought a brand new set of clippers and hid them in my toiletries/underwear drawer only to discover after three consecutive bath times that they had mysteriously disappeared.

Since my bathroom doesn't fall into the area of the Bermuda Triangle I made discreet but unfruitful enquiries, and eventually stooped so low as to search their tackle boxes when they were out. As a result of this underhanded act I uncovered evidence of theft, which had previously been hotly disputed and accompanied by wide-eyed innocence.

I became accustomed to various items of household equipment being purloined and used for their fishing trips and under normal circumstances I didn't mind too much because, sooner or later, quite a bit of it was returned only slightly the worse for wear. Some of it was never seen again, of course, but it wasn't a big deal.

Then it got personal, like the brand new instant Polaroid camera bought for me by the CA as a rare birthday present, he often didn't bother – or just 'forgot'. I'd used it just once and then he took it out on the charter boat and dropped it over the side. It was by mistake, to be fair; there was no malice aforethought. Then there was the Walkman, a similarly infrequent Christmas present, this time, taken on a fishing trip and 'lost.' I told him not to bother to buy me presents in future, especially those that he seemed to want for himself; there didn't seem to be any point. He took me at my word, sadly, and I was given money in an envelope at Christmas thereafter.

So, I bought some new toenail clippers and kept them in the household tool kit with all the DIY tools and wall-papering/painting equipment. I knew they'd be safe in there!

Talking to the animals

So, do carp have a degree of intelligence, then? I know a lady who seems to think that she can communicate with a particular carp and she is not the only angler I know who believes this. I've seen captured carp calm down considerably as they wait for the photo-shoot, because the captor has stuck a thumb in the fish's mouth while uttering endearments and words of comfort.

It's a well-known fact that carp can be perverse. They can swim around for hours, weaving patterns in the water while pretending to be hungry and foraging for food, so that anglers become excited and send out freebie boilies in an effort to tempt them to the bait. The carp are not hungry; we fishing widows know that. How can they be? There is always enough free bait chucked in to feed an aquarium.

As soon as the anglers have their attention distracted from the water's edge by other things, though, a carefully prepared picnic, a pause in proceedings to have a cup of tea, the carp all grab a hook each and mayhem ensues. Time and time again, I've witnessed this phenomenon from my observation post on the bank. It happens far too often for it to be mere coincidence.

Do you know where the carp live?

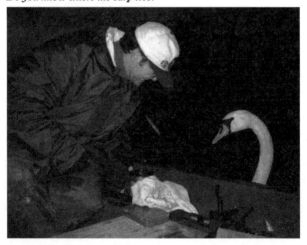

Carp are bait teasers, too. They will circle a floating boilie or flavoured biscuit and nudge it a couple of times to make the angler think he is in with a chance. Who says carp can't give sidelong glances? Then, with a certain nonchalance, they swim away in the opposite direction, then return and repeat the process a number of times before 'oh, go on then,' taking the hook.

They tell me that I have the memory cycle of a goldfish, that's about 30 seconds, but maybe, the bigger the 'goldfish' the longer the memory. Who knows? Has anyone actually proved that oriental carp who come swimming as soon as priests ring the dinner bell are only victims of instinctive behaviour patterns? Perhaps they like the hands that feed them and go to socialise as well as to eat.

Male, logically-brained anglers will dismiss this piece of nonsense as pure fantasy but think on. You don't know for sure, do you?

Stranger than fiction

Some time ago, Chris Tarrant very kindly sent me a snippet for inclusion in the October section of this book. I'd told him that I was looking for strange happenings and he's experienced several! One of them is as follows:

Chris was packing up from fishing one evening just as it was beginning to get dark, at a nice little pool in Hertfordshire, tucked away in a wood. It was a beautiful summer evening, with a great, red sun setting on the horizon and the promise of a clear, starry night.

"I'd had a very successful day," CT related. "Hadn't seen another soul since early morning and was wandering contentedly back through the trees listening to the birdsong. As I rounded a small bush, the sight of a female face broke my reverie. It was staring up at me in horror, from the path, and peering around the back of a man's head. Between them, they wore absolutely nothing. I don't know who was more surprised, them or me."

There's more. "Although this kind of thing keeps happening to me whenever I get my tackle out, it's not the sort of thing I can ever quite get used to and, obviously, they couldn't handle the situation either. Without a word passing between us in the gathering dusk, they abruptly uncoupled - inflicting God knows what kind of damage on each other - and, not bothering to pick up any of their clothes, with their bits and pieces dangling out all over the place, went rushing up the path. Somewhere in the distance, I heard a car start up and drive away, and if it hadn't been for the little pile of clothes still lying on the path, I'd have thought I'd seen ghosts."

"Driving home, giggling to myself," Chris went on, "I wondered where on earth they had gone to in that state and what they would say if they were stopped by a police car. I had visions of the poor bloke giving it an hour and then, still starkers, trying to sneak back, only to get caught by the extremely short-tempered gamekeeper accompanied by his equally nasty Doberman. I could envisage him crawling back to his lady, still naked, with a botty full of buckshot and bites."

Chris thought no more about it, he said, until the following weekend when he went back to the lake and there, along the little path, piled exactly as they had been on the Tuesday, were the clothes - jeans, jumpers, bra, pants, just like before. Where that couple ever got to, or whether they ever got dressed again, he never found out. The clothes stayed there for another week and then the gamekeeper bunged them on the bonfire.

Dog rose

I was quite flattered when one of my young music pupils told me that she had named her hamster after me. That was okay. The hamster is a blonde, with big brown eyes, high cheek bones and is reasonably attractive. I could handle that. No problem.

On a visit to the club lake, though, I found out that a bedraggled spaniel that guards the entrance also answers to 'Rosie.' She's very friendly and has a nice personality, but she needs a complete make-over and possibly an oil change.

I knew that I'd been looking a little haggard. All those early mornings and late evenings running my taxi service to and from lake and shore take their toll, but when they start naming dogs after you, you know that things have become serious and something has to be done.

Maybe I'd caught spaniel Rosie on a bad day. Maybe she had been up all night chasing rabbits but I booked into a beauty parlour as a precaution - although I've been told that a trip to Lourdes might be more productive.

Mouse detective

While sitting in my computer room, late one night, while typing up the latest best seller, not, I heard a rustling sound coming from a cupboard. 'Can't deal with that now,' I thought, head in sand. 'It's probably a draught or something.' We lived in a Victorian end-terrace and there were always odd noises and creaks going on, not always from the house structure, either, unfortunately. It was a perfectly calm night so I knew that the wind was an unlikely cause, but I was in full flow and at my age, if I stopped to investigate, I'd lose the thread and it could have been days before it came back.

The noise ceased and I carried on. Half an hour later, it started again but I knew a solution to the problem. I'd go and have a bath. By the time I returned, someone else would have dealt with the rustling sound and everything would be hunky-dory. Yeah, like that would happen. The only other person who could possibly have dealt with it was entranced by a square box in another room and wouldn't have moved if a herd of elephants had lumbered between him and the TV screen.

After an hour or more of footling about and procrastination, it dawned on me that there was only one person who would sort out this interruption – me. So, I turned on all the lights, stamped around a bit and moved an armchair away from the cupboard base.

I used to buy crisps by the barrow load. You know the deal; a couple of dozen packets contained in one large bag. I had hidden an unopened pack down by the side of a chair because, at the time, number two son would eat crisps instead of taking the trouble to make a sandwich and he could get through half a dozen packets a day if not reined in. As I picked up the bag, I noticed that a largish hole had been chewed in the side of it. I ripped open the pack, emptied it on to the carpet, and found that my 'lodger' had deprived the family of three – count 'em – three whole packets. Clearly, cheese 'n' onion was the favourite flavour of my intruder because he'd ignore the prawn cocktail, barbecued chicken, and salt and vinegar ones. A certain mouse owed me at least a quid already, and there was no way he was getting any more.

By this time, the CA had dragged himself away from whatever he was watching with a ball in it on TV and had emerged from his cocoon to find out grumpily, 'just what all the racket's about.' I told him that we'd probably got a mouse and that it seemed to be living inside the food cupboard.

The vermin residence was all my fault, of course. I shouldn't have left food in a food cupboard. What was I thinking? "Tch. Fancy leaving it there! You'll have to get a trap tomorrow," he said and wandered kitchenwards aiming for the kettle.

A few minutes later he wandered back again, walked toward me carrying a cup of coffee in one hand and a biscuit in the other. I was quite touched. He knew how hard I was working and had considered the fact that I might be hungry, but I should have known better, I really should. He put the coffee in front of me, then strolled over to the cupboard and placed the biscuit carefully inside, on the floor, for the mouse; an attempt at a condemned mouse's last meal.

The following day, I bought a humane trap and caught Mr Mouse, transported him to a clifftop, to the strains of Eric Clapton on the car's stereo system – it was like a live concert for him – and let him go. I made the trip six times in all, as subsequently, I had to release Mrs Mouse and four of their children.

There is a point to this tale. Space had to be found for a new bivvy, and associated equipment such as bedchairs, sleeping bags and so on, and under the stairs seemed the only place available. There was no way new fishing gear was going into the shed. Was I mad even to suggest such a thing? The few cubic feet of under-stair space was full of fishing paraphernalia already, though, and some of it hadn't seen the light of day for over a decade. It was time to have a clear out.

The CA decided that it would be a good idea if he did this, since he knew that I would have just thrown everything into black sacks and dumped the lot. There could have been something useful in there, he said. As it turned out, there wasn't, but what he did find was an ancient, large, cardboard sack of dog biscuits, which he'd forgotten about for God knows how long.

As he picked it up, the bottom of the sack fell out dispensing biscuits and mouse droppings like you wouldn't believe, all over the hall carpet. At last! Here was something that couldn't possibly be my fault. I hadn't left festering dog biscuits under the stairs, and I lost no time in disclaiming any responsibility. I did go on about it a bit, I know, and it was only a small victory, but I was used to taking the blame for everything that didn't go according to plan and it felt good to be able to deny culpability for once.

I took the last mousechild to the cliffs with a spring in my step the following morning and smiled sweetly at half a dozen suited, city commuters walking the cliff path on their way to the train station. They smiled back, nervously, wondered what I was up to, and when I reached the setting-free point, they stopped to watch and then applauded. I was clearly the highlight of their day. How sad is that!

Safe haven

There were occasions when I just needed to get away from everyone and everything. My marriage was not great and although most of the time I could ignore the signs of disintegration and pretend to myself that everything would be all right, I knew that something would have to give eventually. For a long time, I'd been waiting for my boys to grow up, move out, and become settled before having to make the decision, but still hoping I was wrong, that a miracle would happen and the person I was living with would turn into the man I thought I'd married.

I've always felt at peace when near water, whether it's in extreme weather while walking along the beach, on a cool, misty morning on a riverbank or in high summer beside a lake, and all of those places became sanctuaries for me when things became too hard to bear. I could run away for an hour or two and try to think things through. Strange, how that's so hard to do in the home environment.

One morning near the end of my 30-year marriage, and feeling pretty desperate, I drove to the club lake and was pleased to find the car park empty. I parked up, got out of the car, and began to walk toward the small, tree-enclosed Blue Lagoon. If I'd met anyone, I would have greeted them cheerily and returned to the car park, but I didn't.

It was early in the morning and completely quiet. There was no birdsong, no rustling in the undergrowth, no lowing of cattle or rumbling of farm machinery as usual, and I felt as if I was the only person in the world. It was uncanny, but I was too screwed up to be scared, even though the site of the club lake had been an Iron Age settlement and my imagination had ancient souls telling me that I wasn't the first to be going through emotional pain, and certainly wouldn't be the last. I had no idea regarding the practicalities of changing my life but I knew it couldn't carry on as it was, and I'd come to this magical place in an attempt to find a solution to an intolerable situation. I wasn't holding out too much hope, though, I'd been mulling things over for years and hadn't resolved anything.

It was cold, and a mist was lying across the water, hovering about an inch above it like a theatre curtain that hadn't quite reached the floor. There was an acrid smell of wood smoke in the air, everything was damp; leaves, grass, trees…giving a feeling of strangeness and isolation, and there wasn't a ripple on the water as I sat on a log at the edge of a swim and opened my 'coffee to go' bought at a local café.

The plastic cap creaked as I removed it from the cardboard cup and it made far more noise than it should. The acoustics seemed to have changed but maybe that was because all my senses were heightened, probably because I knew that a decision in the next hour would make or break my life; I'd swear it was more to do with my surroundings, though. It sounds weird, I know, but it was almost as if I was gathering energy from the water and the surrounding trees; quite a spiritual experience for one who had long since rejected any formal religion. I began to sift through past events, alternatives, and possible outcomes and it dawned on me that the only person who could repair my life was me; it takes two people to fix a relationship problem and if one party isn't willing, then it cannot be done. I'd given things a fair go, I concluded. I'd tolerated for a couple of decades, been to various organisations, including Relate – alone, and it was about time I resigned myself to the fact that nothing would change. In fact, it could only get worse. No one was going to come along to take me away from it all. This was something I had to do for myself; a very scary prospect for a variety of reasons that I won't go into here.

I had help. There were a few close friends, they know who they are, and my beloved sons, who got me through it all and although I'm not a religious person, in fact, you don't want to get me started on that subject, I came away from the lake that day with a feeling of resignation, peace, and strength. It was as if I had told all my darkest thoughts and fears and had been given some kind of blessing.

I never went back to the Blue Lagoon. A chapter of my life died that day and to return would have broken the spell.

CHAPTER ELEVEN

NOVEMBER - APPLES AND WET LEAVES

Plain to sea

I know there is a scientific basis for all the talk about global warming but I get really fed up when we hear about every bit of extreme weather being caused by car (or cow) exhaust emissions, or the gases we have in our greenhouses. (I'm joking!) Every few years we get heavy snowfall, flood, heatwave or hurricane, and the news channels go raving mad. It's all we hear about.

One such blip in our normally temperate climate happened a few years ago when a friend of mine, a dedicated carp man, went pike fishing at a Thameside syndicate lake. Just a bit of light relief, you understand. It was a casual affair, nothing serious; carp are his first love. He's a country boy and has lived by, and often in, the waters around Horton and Wraysbury all his life. His knowledge of watercraft, flora, fauna, stars, signs of impending storm, fire, flood and famine (he warns when they are about to run out of things to fry) is impressive, so when he propounds on weather conditions we sit up and take notice – well, some of us do.

Terry had caught four fair-sized pike on this particular morning and was packing up to go home when some fishing mates arrived to set up for a carp session.
"You're not going, are you, Tel?" 'Just Gary' was surprised.
"I'm off," Terry warned. "I've never seen this water level rise by a foot and a half in a few hours. You'll be flooded out by teatime."

Just Gary, Gary Mac and Dave the Plumber were not daunted by a prediction of dire consequences. No rain had fallen for several days and, as far as they were concerned, there was no reason for this forecast to be taken seriously.
"That's all right, my son," said Just Gary. "You poof-out and run home with your tail between your legs. We're staying. We're proper carpers, we are!"

The prophet of doom tried to convince his mates by quoting the unicorn/Noah's ark legend.
"The unicorns ignored the advice, failed to get on to the ark and look what happened to them!"
Just Gary wasn't fazed.
"I've seen everything in 20 years of angling," he responded. "Everything from the drought of '76, heavy snowfalls in the 80s and even Paul Selman buying a round during his Harefield days. There's nothing I

ain't seen, I'm telling you. We'll phone you in the morning, after we've been haulin' all night. You can come and take the photos."

Terry made one last attempt.
"This lake is 12 acres," he said. "There is something seriously wrong. We've had no rain today, the access road is already covered in water and even the owners of the big, posh houses by the river are getting twitchy."

"We'll phone you in the morning, mate. We'll be fine." Just Gary carried on pitching his bivvy.

It turned out to be a cold night with a hard frost. The three stalwarts, huddled together under a brolly, had lit a Coleman double burner and placed it on a lump of wood for stability and to facilitate the making of continuous tea. Gradually, it began to dawn on them that there might be something amiss after all.
"Do you reckon old Tel might have had a point?" Dave the Plumber asked of his companions as the lump of wood, Coleman, and kettle began to float away from them.
"Erm...I think I'll move my bivvy up the bank a bit to higher ground."
Gary Mac sensibly did the same thing, although it may have been more sensible to have packed up and gone home.
Just Gary was adamant. "I'm not moving," he told his partners in crime. "It can't come up much higher than this. My baits are perfectly placed and I know where my landing net is."

By the morning, Just Gary's bivvy was nine inches deep in water. In the wee, small hours he had woken up, noticed the lake creeping into his living quarters, managed to grab bedchair and sleeping bag and get to higher ground before he drowned. Meanwhile, rods, reels, alarms, and everything else were seriously underwater. He slept beneath the stars, exposed to the elements, in sub-zero temperatures until daylight.

"I've had to deal with ants, mice and the occasional rat invading the bivvy, in my time," he is quoted as muttering while retrieving dripping equipment, "but I've never been hassled by duckweed!"

Terry phoned early to see if everyone was all right and on discovering that things were anything but, went into rescue mode, including green wellies, and rushed over to his mates on a mission of mercy. The Fellowship of the Bivvy is legendary among carpers, so the Lord of the Rod Rings didn't think twice about venturing into the unknown.

One of the bailiffs was notified of the calamity and mobilised immediately. He turned up in his 4x4 people carrier and commenced carrying people. The first job, of course, was to rescue the syndicate members, then the stricken property owners whose houses stood adjacent to the lake. Flooded out local residents were ferried to dry land (good PR for the syndicate) and cars were towed from the car park to higher ground before daring to start the engines. At this stage in the game, Dave the Plumber's Fiesta van had water over the top of the bonnet, and one local resident, who owned a multi-million pound house, decided to bugger off to Barbados for a week while the floods subsided in his absence. Clearly, some syndicate waters are in classier areas than others.

The cause of all this mayhem was never officially declared but during the rescue, there were dark mutterings to be heard from formerly loyal subjects, about how certain measures had been taken in order to prevent the Queen's corgis, downriver at Windsor, from having to do the breaststroke on their morning constitutional. The evidence to support this conclusion was discussed at length and accepted as suspicious, at the very least, if not downright sinister. Conspiracy theories abounded.

Despite there having been little rain in the weeks preceding the event, and certainly not sufficient to warrant the extent of the flood, Wraysbury residents were supplied with several thousand sandbags. To give you some idea of the magnitude of water levels, a nearby tackle shop sold 50 pairs of waders in a single day and could have sold another 50, had supplies been forthcoming. Locals had never seen anything like it.

It turns out that there was a flood relief scheme in operation to divert water from the Windsor/Maidenhead area and although this helped the residents of those areas, it swamped everyone else in the vicinity, and ruined an anticipated fine fishing weekend for those daft enough to ignore the advice of a knowledgeable mate.

Clearly, the committee responsible for the relief of Windsor hadn't considered where all the excess water would go, so flood plains around Wraysbury, Staines and Chertsey bore the brunt of this lack of forethought; even Thorpe Park developed several new water features overnight. What had been intended as flood relief turned out to be flood release, and someone had neglected to make the Thames big enough to accommodate the overflow.

There could be an upside, of course. Some of the future catches in the Thames could be quite spectacular. Captive koi and other exotics that escaped their mansion-side pools and swam up high streets into the river proper could be breeding still. There could be all manner of brand new species of carp emerging soon.

I have to mention that all nine of the Fox buzzers, hung in trees along with various articles of clothing, bedding and luggage, worked perfectly once dried out. They had been subjected to an excess of liquid all night and still were able to function the next day. There are a few of us who wish we could do that!

Two weeks later, when the fishing weekend rolled round again, Dave the Plumber and Just Gary, for the first time in their lives took notice of weather forecasts and thought better of venturing lakewards. They need not have bothered with the expert meteorologists, though; they could have just asked Terry if he was going.

Winter rainbow; there's always a silver lining.

Mere trifles

One way to cheer up the family during the cold and dreary winter months, when carp fishing trips began to take on the characteristics of a Japanese game show, was to surprise them with a summer pud. I felt sorry for them. It must have been pretty awful to have no control over the compulsion to venture forth into dire weather conditions as they enjoyed their hobby. The least I could do to compensate for their suffering was to ensure they had a decent meal ready and waiting for when they returned home blank, cold and depressed.

Usually, at this time of the year, any pud involved apples. I had friends who were very generous with windfalls; local apples used to be tuppence-a-ton in friendly greengrocers' shops and I could never pass up a bargain, even if I had a couple of hundredweight of Cox's at home. Freezers were invented so that frugal housewives could take advantage of glut.

Every year, I made soup, ketchup, pizza topping, pasta sauce with July tomatoes and pies, flans, sauce, and chutney with the apple harvest. There came a time, though, when even I thought that one more apple-based dessert would be too much.

Because my life was crammed with so many things to do, I had to think everything through and prepare in advance, so I assembled the ingredients for a luxury trifle the night before and left them in readiness on the kitchen worktop. An extra pinta had already been bought from the all-night grocer, on my way back from railway-station taxi duty.

Raspberry blancmange mix, fresh raspberries, the remains of another surfeit of fruit gathered last summer, carefully frozen and now left to defrost overnight, raspberry jelly and a carton of double cream all waited patiently for my attention the following morning along with a packet of eight trifle sponges. The trifle was as good as made. How pleased they would be, when I offered my family this treat instead of the customary apple crumble and custard.

I had reckoned without number one son. He had returned home at 2am after a pub/curry evening with his mates and they'd decided that there was no point in going to bed since a pre-arranged carp hunting trip was due to kick off at 6am. Why wait for daylight? They were going to start now. I heard him crashing about in the kitchen, removing boilies from the freezer, and making groundbait out of stale bread, kept expressly for the purpose, breakfast cereal, and whatnot. You know what's coming, don't you?

The following morning when I went to construct my state-of-the-art trifle, there were just two miniscule trifle sponges left in the packet. The others had been added to the groundbait mix.

"Why leave two?" I asked him when he returned that evening. Apparently, the logic behind it was that if he'd taken them all I would have spent ages looking for them, what with my dodgy memory and all, thinking that I'd mislaid them somewhere. See what I mean? There is no rhyme or reason for the way they think.

I forgave the thief because he was very appreciative of the raspberry crumble and cream that I knocked up instead.

Another way to combat early winter blues is the occasional fritter. "What?" I hear anglers cry. "We only use Spam for bait. We'll chuck it in a lake but wouldn't dream of eating it ourselves. During the war..." I don't mean the fried-in-batter variety of fritter. I'm talking about the wastage of a small amount of money, say a tenner, on things that fishing widows could really do without.

The CA used to express mild irritation when I returned from visits to boot sales or the 'Everything Under a Quid' shops, but it made me feel so much better, so I occasionally risked his displeasure. Besides, he went fishing when he needed cheering up, and it wasn't his money I was spending.

One particularly fruitful foray into the world of tat produced a plaster birdhouse for 99p intended for the amusement of a couple of blue tits that visited my bay tree on a regular basis in search of food. "What on earth do you want that for?" He was right, of course; the tits had managed perfectly well without a mobile home. He sneered at a packet of rubbers for 50p (the kind that erase pencil marks, do try to concentrate) and two miniscule picture frames for which you'd need a microscope if you wanted to see the locket-sized photos inside.

A shiny, canary-yellow alarm clock, however, bought because the existing one rang whenever it felt like it and never at the time we wanted to get out of bed, met with the Chief Angler's complete approval.
"Great," he said. "Now I don't have to worry about missing the tide/being late at the lake."

So, girls, I reckon I've cracked it. If you can relate everything you waste money on to angling, you'll get away with it - until they cotton on and suggest you fritter in the tackle shop, that is.

Carp for lunch?

Hugh Fearnley–Whittingstall came in for some flack when he caught, cooked, and consumed a wild common carp during one of his 'live off the land for absolutely no expenditure whatsoever' programmes on TV.

There were howls of protest from carpers countrywide, all of them declaring that this kind of anti-social behaviour shouldn't be allowed. I was puzzled at first but then the penny dropped. The only explanation for this outcry must be that carp, to carp anglers, become familiar. They are akin to pets; they're given names, revered, respected, and loved.

I know of people who kept orphaned piglets or lambs as members of the family and they had a similar way of thinking. They wouldn't dream of eating their friends, despite the fact that these animals are generally accepted as more often seen on a butcher's slab. Even dogs are consumed in some parts of the world and horse is surprisingly sweet and tender. I only ate horse once and by mistake; I assumed it was beefsteak until enlightened after the evidence had been committed to stomach.

Being part of a circle of friends who go sea fishing almost as regularly as they sit beside still water, I was called upon to cook and eat the fruits of every sea trip and very tasty they were, too, so I've often wondered about the possible culinary value of a fine carp. I hasten to add that it's only a mild curiosity.

For obvious reasons, I wouldn't dare consider carrying out my fantasies through.

Our local Chinese take-away proprietor positively slavered over photographs of captured specimens. These were shown to him with pride on a regular basis and intended as proof of angling prowess only, as one or other of my menfolk waited in his shop for their supper to be prepared. Once, to my anglers' collective horror, Mr Fong offered me a recipe for carp, steamed in a wok with scallions, ginger and fish stock, which I politely wrote down and discarded immediately we had left his establishment to a chorus of, "You're not actually gonna do that? How could you? Well, I'm not eating it!" This while they were clutching a bag containing prawn dumplings, sweet and sour pig, and chicken balls; carp's a fish, isn't it? Food.

Don't show 'em to Mr Fong...

...white wine, mushrooms, single cream...

Carp are eaten as a matter of course in the Eastern Bloc, all points oriental, and they used to be eaten in this country. They still would be if groups of asylum seekers could succeed in getting away with it. A perfectly natural assumption for them is that the fish are there to be caught, hoiked out of the lakes or rivers, and taken home to feed the family. It's done in their own country, why not here? They have no idea that it's a crime and that they're poaching. Surprised by the strong reaction they receive from lake bailiffs, they go home disappointed and confused by our strange, English customs.

Our local wet fish shop sells carp for the religious holiday feasts of our Jewish community. These are 'farmed carp, expressly for the purpose,' I was told, so that's acceptable. They haven't been held by an adoring angler and photographed; therefore, they can be cooked and devoured. The Victorian Mrs Beeton offered recipes for stewed or baked carp so there should be no surprise that a quite hungry TV cook might fry one to a crisp at the riverside.

Anglers were worried sick, apparently, because Mr Fearnley-Whittingstall seemed to be advocating the catching and cooking of carp and they imagined that the stocks in our lakes and rivers would be sadly depleted as a rush of would-be consumers arrived at the waterside. We know, though, don't we, that there was no cause for alarm. Mr F-W is not a dedicated carp man and doesn't understand the way of things. It's all very well him telling others to go out and do the same but you've got to catch 'em first, before you can cook them. Judging by my own anglers and the ratio of blank days to fruitful ones, we'd all starve, wouldn't we?

Espresso love

A friend of mine is a tackle tart. He denies it, of course, and normally I'm not moved by his demonstrations of amazing gadgetry, most of which is designed to save time and effort at a water's edge but, in fact, makes a task take twice as long by the time the whole thing's been set up and written instructions obeycd.

Having said that, I attended a weekend fish-in and found myself impressed by his latest acquisition. "Fancy a coffee, Rosie?" he asked as soon as I arrived at his swim, knowing that I never turn down the offer of caffeine, and proceeded to go through the motions with a certain of flourish and flair, it has to be said.

Minutes later, I was handed a small, green cup containing four fluid ounces (a couple of mouthfuls) of dark brown liquid. I was slightly disappointed; coffee, to me, is a large, steaming mug full of the stuff. Then I tasted it. It was pure heaven, strong and black espresso.

I made myself a nuisance for the rest of the weekend, demanded espresso whenever the kick from the last one had worn off, and determined to get hold of one of those magic little machines for myself.

My coffee maker goes everywhere with me now. I can fit it into a handbag and providing I can find an angler with a heat source, there is no need for me to disturb my fishing mates with unreasonable demands at inconvenient times. I've even used it at home when I'm fed up. A cup of espresso with a Cadbury's flake dipped into it, sucked slowly until it dissolves in the mouth is better than anything – well, nearly anything – I know.

Super-maggot

I have a theory that maggot breeders countrywide are huddled in darkened laboratories, casting surreptitious glances over their shoulders as they secretly experiment with a new strain; a maggot for all seasons, a maggot to take over the world.

Every Friday afternoon for years, I went into my local tackle dealer and asked for 'a pint of mixed, please, but make sure that the little thin red ones are on the top.' Don't ask me why this was so important, I don't know why. I just did as I was asked. It didn't seem to matter, anyway, because whatever the position of the little red ones at the outset, they wiggled their way to the top in a matter of minutes.

Our maggot boxes were just the ordinary, run-of-the-mill type, square with a lid containing minute air holes. I discovered, though, over a matter of weeks that the little red jobbies are capable of squeezing their thin bodies through these air vents. Then, jumping out, wriggling across the bottom of a bucket, hauling themselves up the side and on reaching the top, base-jumping themselves over the rim into the unknown – a no-maggots land that to them must be far below. Reminiscent of how it must have been in the trenches, I could imagine the leaders waiting for their troops to catch up before one gave the signal, "Over the top, boys. Let's show this fishing widow what we're made of. Good luck everybody. See you in Blighty."

A Medusa of maggots.

In nearly every room we had cheap, corded carpet for the simple reason that I lived with anglers. If the floor coverings became too badly stained with mud, worm juice, or stagnant river water, they could be replaced and easily laid by me, for 20 quid or so. I was far too lazy to nag as a preventative measure (I did try it once but it wore me out and no one took any notice, anyway), so this was a good way of ensuring reasonably clean floors. The grooves in these carpets, however, provided excellent cover for escaping maggots.

Once safely landed in the hallway, they couldn't possibly lose all sense of direction because the weave of the floor covering automatically channelled them either toward the kitchen or the front door. From a distance and without my glasses it looked as if the hallway carpet had developed pink stripes overnight, moving ones at that. It can be pretty disconcerting first thing in the morning before a caffeine kick-start. I was not allowed to vacuum them, either, not until every possible escapee had been gently retrieved and replaced – not by me, as if you needed to be told. Only when my anglers were certain that no more could be rescued was I let loose with the Hoover.

After one particularly satisfying maggot skirmish when my anglers were all at work, I just vacuumed the lot, intending to buy more from the tackle shop later and replace the runaways. I had cleaned the hallway and sat down with a cuppa, then realised that if I didn't empty the cleaner bag there and then, in a couple of weeks or so, after metamorphosis, it could start to move of its own accord. My house was similar to the twilight zone as it was; a self-motivated vaccuum cleaner was the last thing I needed.

Those thin, red maggots must have had extraordinary powers of survival for, despite the cleaning onslaught inflicted upon the carpets and surrounding areas, we still had a mini-invasion of airborne troops which were small, green and had to be regularly released through the back door. I just waited for the summer months. With their talent for escapology, there was no way they were going to be let loose in my fridge and since maggots had, in previous years, taken precedence over the family's chilled food, I could see trouble looming. Cries of, "What's the matter with you? Maggots are clean!" would fall on deaf ears. Did they know how and what grown-up maggots consume? Any fly stupid enough to venture into my house was and still is zapped immediately before it can vomit over anything I'm likely to touch.

Eventually, they bought their own fridge and installed it in the shed, moaning about the unreasonable attitude of fishing widows/mothers all the time they were doing it, but I ignored the criticism. If I couldn't see the maggots, I didn't care where their sense of adventure took them.

What's in a name?

I visited a lake recently that had every swim named with its own little wooden plaque. How quaint, I thought, but it set me thinking. How do the names get thought up in the first place? I asked a couple of fishing mates about it.

It turns out that several lakes have a swim called the Willows, for obvious reasons and most have the Car Park, because it's the one nearest to the lake entrance. However, on investigation I found that many others have names that have been invented by anglers who, I can only assume, are either bored out of their wits or under the influence of some substance or other when they think them up.

Some are logical. Dead Man's I can accept because there really was a body hauled out of this particular swim, a few years back. The Hide is OK, too, as it's hidden behind reeds and shrubbery, and The Mud because it's the only swim devoid of all vegetation. Others, though, need hallucinogenic influence in order to establish a connection.

The Witch so called, I was told, because it is situated adjacent to a willow vaguely shaped as a pointy hat and a warty chin. There's a limit to the amount of imagination required in an attempt to see that one, especially if it's a windy day. Then there's the Squid which name, I am reliably informed, comes from a dead alder which has half a dozen branches in a kind of fan arrangement that looks as if a squid has crash-landed on top of it. How bored do anglers get, for goodness sake?

I liked Sanctuary; it smacked of peace and quiet, a bolthole where a fishing widow could sit and stare, or read in tranquillity. Then they told me that the name was not for the benefit of anglers who fished there; had I not noticed that there was no shelter from the elements, not even a solitary tree? It was named because the carp used it as a place of refuge where they could hide under the lily pads.

I came up with a few others that make far more sense. How about Blankers? The Somnambulist, for anglers who need sufficient room to fall out of a bivvy in the wee, small hours to land their prize while still half asleep. The Insomniac - a smaller swim for those who refuse to sleep at all. The Tree of Plenty, dominated by a tall oak decorated with various items of tackle cast in the dark and impaled upon the trunk. Here for the Weekend - so don't bother waiting for me to pack up so you can move in, and one for every lake is surely, I'm Sitting Here but Fishing Over There.

See? Much more interesting than the Willows, aren't they?

CHAPTER TWELVE

DECEMBER - YULE BE SORRY

Festive fishing and reflections

Christmas, when young anglers were around, I realised early on, had to be approached from a different standpoint to previous festive seasons that I had known and loved.

Gone were the days when I could wrap up a 'Beano' annual and those chocolate coins in gold mesh bags to put in their stockings. As they grew up and discovered the joys of angling, the Christmas goal posts moved and stocking fillers had to be connected, however tenuously, to their passion in life. Books entitled 'How to Catch a Big One' or 'How to Persuade Your Mother that Every Bit of Tackle in the Shop is Vital to Your Existence' would have been accepted with glee.

As it was, I insisted that they each hang up a Christmas stocking, more for my own delight than theirs. I know that they only agreed to it to keep me on an even keel but a great deal of pleasure was derived from pretending that were still infants rather than anglers.

The contents of these stockings had to be identical, though, and the weight evenly distributed. You may be able to wrap each item in different coloured papers but if you lovingly place several containers of small shot or half a dozen weights into a long, white wader sock and then try to hang it up, it will touch the floor however high you can reach. I knew from experience that if one stocking were half a centimetre longer than the other there would be a punch-up on Christmas morning.

The 'real' presents were chosen with care and instructions given to fond grandparents, uncles, aunts, and family friends that everything had to have angling connotations. I could not, for example, purchase a watch that did not incorporate at least the phases of the moon and if possible the state of the tides. Cameras had to be capable of adding the time and date to every print so that captures could be recorded for posterity. Clothing had to be in nature's colours, even down to underpants. If they couldn't use it/look at it while fishing, they weren't interested.

By necessity, Christmas dinner had to be served in the early evening instead of 2pm, as in years gone by. One Christmas morning, they went fishing off the wharf to try out the new rod/reel and came home plastered because a local charter boat skipper had offered them seasonal cheer. Even the youngest, deemed old enough to accompany his father and brother for the first time, looked slightly green about the gills. He wasn't old enough to drink yet but was going through the 'see how many chocolate bars I can cram in before I'm sick' stage and had consumed a couple of Selection packs that he'd taken along in case he felt peckish on the beach.

I knew they wouldn't be recovered enough to face turkey and trimmings until the evening and, in any case, my priority was to wash their clothes. Leave them for longer than 12 hours and no amount of air-freshener can disguise the stench of stale seawater.

When they eventually made it to the table, having been sleeping it off all afternoon, I made it a rule that the conversation did not include a verbal action replay of the morning events. There should be at least one day of the year when a fishing widow is not expected to show enthusiasm, after the twentieth repetition, for the capture of a small flounder.

After dinner, when traditionally we used to play Junior Trivial Pursuit, Buckeroo or create the Air-Fix kits bought by fond aunties, we had fishing rods and reels stripped down on newspaper all over the dining room floor. It was imperative, they told me, that the tools of their trade be cleaned, oiled and tucked up for the night, for they would be needed first thing in the morning. Angling appetites, once whetted, must be assuaged at any cost and Boxing Day was for fishing. Why else would turkey sandwiches have been invented?

Christmas at sea.

Christmas casualty

Why is it that if a youngster is going to need hospital treatment, it always happens during a bank holiday? The rest of the year is accident free but the number of times I've spent bank holidays in the casualty department of our local hospital defies accounting.

My sons always favoured the days leading up to Christmas as the ideal time to have emergency treatment. We were on first name terms with most of the casualty staff, anyway, because the eldest suffered with chronic asthma and was in and out of hospital like a yo-yo, and there were some Yuletides when we were greeted like old friends whenever we put in an appearance.

One year, I had refused to allow them to go fishing on Christmas Eve. There was always a great deal to do and I hadn't the time to chauffeur them to the lakes and back. After an hour of disgruntled telephone calls, explaining to friends about 'the old crone who'd suddenly got religion', the boys eventually managed to persuade another mother to lend her car to the eldest of the group who had just passed his test. They set of with a 'See! We don't need you' attitude to have a look at some local carp that were in the throes of an unseasonable feeding frenzy, or so someone with a vivid imagination had reported. Off they went into the wilds, well, as wild as you can get in Essex, armed with just a dozen cans of fizzy drink and quite a bit of the Christmas stash of goodies, purloined just in case they got lost and had to survive more than an hour without sugar.

They brought him home in the early afternoon, a previously clean white T-shirt draped tastefully, if blood sodden, over his right hand. They were all worried but the most panic stricken of the stretcher-bearers was the driver of the borrowed car, desperate to find out how to get bloodstains from his mother's upholstery. Never mind his friend who might have been bleeding to death, he was after saving his own skin.

Apparently, number one son had shinned up a number of trees in order to get a better view of the almost inanimate and comatose carp and then overconfidently, he had thrown himself out of the last tree, hoping to land panther-like and 'cool' among admiring mates. In fact, he had landed awkwardly and thrust out his hands to save his face from being smashed in. Unfortunately, he had chosen a picnicking site for his landing place and the broken bottle with which his hand had come into contact had left a deep gash along the length of a finger that still bled profusely after half an hour of frantic staunching with the T-shirt.

We trundled off on one of our customary trips to hospital, but as loss of teenage blood is not classed as an emergency, we waited for some time while the more serious injuries trooped past us, mostly the result of pre-Christmas festivities. The place was crawling with police, who were fielding the victims of alcohol-induced violence and stupidity as they ricocheted tipsily out of treatment cubicles. One jolly sergeant had tinsel round his cap, augmented by fairy lights powered by a battery inside his tunic. Who says our police have no sense of humour?

By the time the eldest was ushered into Sister's cubbyhole, the feeling had returned to his wound and he was in some discomfort. They always ask how it happened, don't they? Sister had clearly heard so many 'how it happened' stories that she'd had enough. Her face became frosty as our particular tale was unfolded and as the explanation petered out, she launched into a lecture on the stupidity of propelling oneself from high places without the benefit of a parachute, and the dangers of playing the fool. We tried to explain that he hadn't been playing at anything; the stalking of carp is a serious business, but she wasn't having any so we gave up.

"It will have to be stitched," Sister told us tersely, looking as if she'd quite like to do it herself with a sail-maker's needle and garden twine. We almost began to feel sorry for the lager louts; their wounds would amount to nothing compared to sister's recriminations. So, after a student nurse had cleaned and stitched and everyone, bar Sister, had wished us a Merry Christmas, we were allowed to leave.

I felt so guilty. Well, it was my fault, in a way. If I had allowed him to go fishing at the local lake as he usually did, he wouldn't have felt the urge to climb trees. I let them go on Boxing Day and after that, it remained as a tradition, year after year. I'm convinced he did it deliberately.

Initiative

Everyone should carry a Coleman stove in the boot of the car, particularly if you either don't belong to a motoring organisation or have a habit of forgetting your mobile phone. I knew a young, dedicated carp angler (I still do but now he's a much older, dedicated carp angler) who used to leave a complete set of tackle and equipment in his boot, just in case he happened by a pool of water that looked as if it might be worth a look. Sometimes it worked, too. He caught several carp by the opportunist method.

Trev's 13lb 8oz mirror.

One cold and frosty night before the advent of mobile phones, he was driving along country roads when his car ran out of petrol. He didn't panic because he was stranded on his own in the dark and the nearest village with a public phone was at least two miles away. Instead, he walked calmly to the boot, retrieved the Coleman, undid his petrol cap, unscrewed the filler-cap on the Coleman, and upended it into the petrol tank. This, added to the quarter of a gallon spare fuel intended to refill the Coleman, provided just enough petrol to get him to the nearest service station.

Now, that's what I call innovative thinking.

Indoor fishing

Rarely, there was a Christmas when the entire festival was not dominated by fishing. There will always be moments, of course, like Christmas lunchtime and the opening of presents containing thermal socks, vests and long-johns, a new reel or two, videos and anglers' diaries, but there could be a man-flu virus, going around, the kind that induces severe bouts of self-pity among the male population.

One Yuletide when we had this dire consequence inflicted upon us, my anglers felt so poorly for the duration that they sat in front of Sky TV on a diet of John Wilson, Andy Little and Screaming Reels repeats, washed down with their favourite alcoholic beverages. It was hell on earth for me, I might tell you.

Apart from the regular assertions that 'fishing makes you hungry', especially when it's from the comfort of an armchair, I had to wear my Florence Nightingale hat. You know what men are like when they're off colour. They can endure a serious illness or a major operation with fortitude and a minimum of complaint but give 'em a head cold and they think they're dying.

Because they didn't all get it at once and there was a couple of days overlap of the direst symptoms, I seemed to spend a whole week gravitating between TV room and kitchen. Apparently, I was in charge of bearing trays of comforting dishes; hot soup to ease their shivers, lemon and honey for their sore throats and, as they began to feel better but wouldn't let on for fear of the room service being curtailed, more substantial platefuls of proper food.

I fell foul to the cold on New Year's Eve and had to make my own arrangements for comfort food and hot toddies. They'd all buggered off fishing.

Mother of all anglers

I have been accused of being 'everybody's mother'. A fair comment, I guess, since most of the anglers I mix with treat me as such. This has nothing to do with my having reached 'a certain age' either; it was always thus, even when I was young. I have no idea why I provoke this reaction. Maybe it's because I'm at my happiest when looking out for my companions, making sure they are well fed, comfortable, and entertained, or perhaps I've always looked old. I was told that I looked 'mumsy' when I was 24 and single.

Like I said, I have no idea why 99% of the men I know react to me this way but I am about to milk it. So, taking advantage of my over-developed maternal instinct, I feel entitled, as universal anglers' mum and purely for their own good, to point out a few things. Fishing mothers and widows should take note and pass on these pearls of wisdom to their own anglers.

Firstly, I wish they'd take care what they're doing when armed with a bait-needle. If you get the opportunity, watch them when they are about to re-bait. They will do the following, I guarantee.

1. Take boilie stop off hair.
2. Place stop in mouth, even when covered in something really unspeakable, because it is so small it might blow away and/or they'd never find it again if they put it anywhere else.
3. Take old boilie off hook.
4. Thread new boilie on to hook with bait-needle.
5. They now have the hook/boilie in one hand and the bait-needle in the other. Brain is concentrating on the next step. It is consumed with the need to boilie stop.
6. Take boilie stop out of mouth, preparatory to securing the boilie, with the same hand containing the bait-needle.
7. Miss iris of eye by a gnat's, thus narrowly avoiding visit to casualty - this time.

Put the needle down!

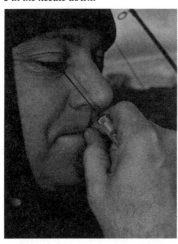

I've seen three separate anglers do this, recently, and it's so dangerous. When I have uttered warnings of dire consequence, the anglers in question had no idea they were doing it, so don't tell me that they never do. I don't believe it. Watch them; I'll bet you 50p it happens.

And another thing…I've also seen anglers slipping and sliding down steep banks in sub-zero temperatures, inches away from freezing water. They are generally wearing heavy boots, Michelin layers of clothing and would have no chance of clambering out again in a hurry if they fell in.

I know of one young man who had to spend the day wrapped in a borrowed fleece and an ancient dog's blanket, hurriedly retrieved from the back seat of his car. He had fallen in and soaked every item of clothing he wore but couldn't possibly yield to common sense by leaving the lake for a couple of hours and return home for dry clothes. That would be giving in and he's a bloke. They don't do that kind of thing.

After number one son had left home, I was pleased to find among the detritus in his shambles of a bedroom,

Good grub. Who needs plates!

Salmonella sausage, anyone?

a photo of him eating a full English fry-up. He was scooping it from a frying pan with a filleting knife, but at least he'd cooked something. Mind you, I hadn't been shown the photo previously; he knew I'd have a go at him about using the knife when he'd got half the kitchen cutlery drawer in his rucksack – and hold on a minute – that frying pan was the new one that mysteriously disappeared.

I worry about what they eat - yes, I'm still on that crusade - and the irregular times that they do it. Having a huge meal washed down by an excess of alcohol just before they crash out on a bedchair for the night is not a great idea; and they wonder why they feel sluggish and confused in the morning? Replacing a fish into the margins, into diluted rat's urine, and then reaching for a salmonella and cucumber sandwich is not a great idea either. If I'm in charge of the catering, we eat an early, full English breakfast, lunch at one and dinner at six.

While on the subject of food, during the short time that I became obsessed with trying to be a proper angler, I tried to experience everything that proper anglers do, even what I consider to be the extreme things like going without hot water and perfumed foam for more than a couple of days. I've even been known to wash my hair in cold water and let it dry, poker straight, in sunlight without a vestige of conditioner or mousse. I've done most things al fresco so the time had come, I thought, to approach the final frontier and get to grips with the proper angler's favourite repast - the Pot Noodle.

At every venue I visited, there was at least one stricken angler waiting for the time when the 1% desperation for food overtook the 99% fishing part of the brain. This desperation factor has to be the only conclusion I can come to, for the Pot Noodle is singularly the most disgusting item of food that has ever passed my lips, and I've eaten some weird stuff at a water's edge, let me tell you.

It didn't look too bad on the pack. The illustration showed a piping hot conglomeration of noodles, chunks of 'chicken', various, colourful vegetables and a shiny sauce. I carefully avoided reading the ingredients panel. Once rehydrated, the resulting mess gave me a distinct impression that someone else had already eaten and ejected it. It tasted of monosodium glutamate, smelled strongly of chemicals and the texture was soft and slimy.

I dare say I'm going to have the Pot Noodle manufacturers throwing bricks through my window, or at the very least suing for libel, although I hardly think that my opinion is going to put them out of business, but I just have to ask why any of you subject your digestive tracts to this pseudo-pasta.

Is it because it's the ultimate convenience food and only takes a few minutes to prepare, you don't need to cook it, and you enjoy eating unrecognisable slop? What? Please, those of you perform this 'potty' ritual; publish your reasons on a forum somewhere. I am genuinely puzzled. The vast majority of anglers I know, enjoy eating as much as fishing and I can't work out why anyone would prefer to eat something factory produced from a plastic pot when, in ten minutes they could have real pasta with a decent sauce.

To please me, I beg you to try this. It's so simple and you won't be hungry again after half an hour, as I was after my Pot Noodle experience. I only ate half of it, though. I was hoping that it might improve if I persevered, but when it didn't, I stopped. That might have had something to do with the hunger issue, to be fair.

Anyway, for a really tasty and filling meal, all you have to do is to boil salted water in a smallish saucepan. Add a few handfuls of penne/rigatoni pasta. Boil it for ten minutes, and then drain off the water. Add a Dolmio stir-in sauce to the pasta, swish it around a bit, and scatter grated cheese over the top. You can even eat it from the pan, if you like. Better still, knock up a Bolognese sauce at home, and freeze it in portions so you can grab one or two as you run out of the door toward the lake. It's so simple; Bolognese sauce takes 30 minutes to prepare and you could make enough to last several weeks. At a water's edge, you just shove it into the drained pasta, add a knob of butter and heat through for a minute or two. It's wonderful, I promise you.

Be warned. Eating stuff like Pot Noodle is not normal behaviour for a proper angler. It is not proper anglers' food. If you see me walking round a lake and you have a PN about your person, I shall have to come over all strict and confiscate it!

Most anglers think that they know the most important things about carp fishing; bait, tackle, finding the fish, technique, and welfare of the carp. They buy the recommended sized mesh landing net, soft and squishy unhooking mats, Klinik for the carp's poorly bits and barbless hooks. They take care not to overload the fish with particles, speak to them gently as they hold them

Now, that's what I call a sarnie!

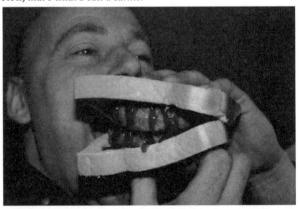

ready for release and generally treat them with respect, but the most important aspect of any kind of outdoor pursuit is returning home safely.

Fishing widows unite. Make a stand. Knock 'em into shape and insist that they look after themselves and their companions. Er…I've just realised that to do this means that you'd probably have to go with them and that's a bit over the top. Okay then, just give them a kiss, tuck them in, and read them this story.

Brownie points

One of the Sunday tabloids reported a story about a woman who divorced her carp angler husband because he used a pair of her tights in which to dry out his boilies. The woman was incensed, apparently, and said the inappropriate use of her best tights was the last straw that broke the back of their marriage. She couldn't cope, she said, with her angler's strange habits, besides him going fishing all the time and leaving her on her own.

I can't understand any woman who divorces just because her partner goes fishing, unless she is so dense that she has no interests of her own, or so self-centred that she wants her mate's full attention and his world to rotate around her alone. She should be pleased that the man in her life is a happy, occupied angler. In fact, I don't believe that fishing is the underlying reason behind the breakdown of any angling partnership. It must be that an angler gambles excessively and then goes fishing, or beats her up when he comes home from fishing, or commits adultery during the rare moments that he's not fishing, or something along those lines.

I'd really like to know what makes certain women tick. What makes some of us think that we are so important that we are entitled to give orders to another individual, whether we are married to them, or not. I've heard anglers – and not just anglers – when asked to go on a jaunt by their mates say, "Better not. I won't get away with it again. I went last week," or simply, "The wife won't let me." So what's all this 'let' business, then? I wouldn't want my partner, if I had one, to tell me I wasn't allowed to visit a cinema with a friend or read my stack of library books. Living with someone shouldn't give us the right to lay down laws.

Every one of us has something we enjoy doing that probably takes up a good proportion of our time. Just looking round my own family and friends I've uncovered a multitude of interests that could be classed as verging on the obsession; golf, horses, cars, shopping, dressmaking, housework – yes, there is one, very sad – snooker, DIY, fishing...and why not? Why create hassle by making life difficult for others? We get enough strife from sources beyond our control as it is, and besides, life's too short.

I know that many of my friends and acquaintances think I'm weird and they're not entirely wrong, but I began to develop a way of thinking a long time ago. One clear night, on the way back from a three-year stay in Australia, my late father took me on to the top deck of an ocean-going liner and asked me to tell him what I could see. I was 18; what I could see was glowing, phosphorescent water, an attractive sailor or several and the opportunity for romance. We were in the middle of the Indian Ocean, four days out of Fremantle with another four days sailing ahead of us before we hit landfall at Sri Lanka.

"Look up," said my father, pointing at a clear sky dotted with a squillion stars; it seemed that I could reach out and touch it. "That vastness is just a small part of the universe. Imagine it millions of times over and you'll understand that, relatively, we are all insignificant beings. As you grow up you may be tempted to consider yourself the most important person in your world, but be aware that other folk have feelings, too; always put yourself in their shoes. Think of what you've seen tonight, it will help you to keep your feet on the ground." A profound thinker was my dad.

There was quite a bit more dialogue between us on that night, but in a nutshell, he was telling me to put others before myself, not to be self-centred, be modest and unassuming, to consider other people and not expect to be treated as anything special by anyone. I tried to live by that and in hindsight, I'm not sure that all of his advice was the best for me, but all that aside, if a bloke wants to spend all his waking and not working moments trying to catch anything that swims and he is happy, I can't see the problem with that. Tolerance level of other people's personality traits depends on the way you look at life.

I was rattling on about all this while sitting by a campfire with a bottle of port and some fishing mates who agreed with most of my views, or so they said. It provoked a discussion, though, about how anglers could impress their womenfolk, should they need to. None of the assembled party would ever need to, obviously, but suppose they did?

"It's no good asking me," I replied, when asked for tips and tricks. "I could never see the point of all that nonsense." If the CA wanted to go fishing, he just went. There was no haggling involved. We didn't split up because he had an all-consuming pastime – not that particular one, anyway.

The object of the brownie point exercise is to ensure fishing weekends away from home on a regular basis without all the hassle of begging and pleading, not that my friends ever had to do that, they kept repeating. The subject, apparently, dominates the thoughts of some male anglers for several minutes of every hour they spend fishing. In an effort to wangle the next weekend bivvied up by a lake without snorts of disapproval and cries of 'what about me?' they have to think ahead.

I had no idea that this was an issue in many households. I had no problem at all with the CA's desire to go fishing at every opportunity. It seemed perfectly normal at the time, and it's only in retrospect that I realise just how much 'man's work' I actually did while he was not around. It wasn't until my companions began to list ways in which they obtained Brownie points that I cottoned on. In the past, it appeared that I had accrued sufficient points to keep me in weekend fishing trips for the rest of my days!

The big ones, I was told, where not only points were earned but badges too, were as follows:

The engagement party weekend. (I couldn't relate to that, didn't get one of those).

The wedding. No fishing was allowed, they said, for the week before the nuptials or during the fortnight afterwards on honeymoon. I won't go into detail but my 'honeymoon' lasted three days before it all got too much for my new husband and he went fishing with his mates – and that was only because his mates had been too busy to go earlier. Mind you, I was glad for him to go even then. I wanted him to be happy. I'm just amazed that there are women who would have created merry hell.

Then there are the non-fishing holidays; apparently, there are such things. These must be tolerated in exchange for a peaceful weekend beside water, although if the holiday is for more or less than a week, the fishing weekends are worked out pro rata.

The suggested purchase of a family car, pretty to look at but totally unsuitable for the carriage of mountains of fishing gear was tentatively discussed, and finally rejected as a Brownie point too far. My ex-angler didn't drive but I always seemed to be persuaded into ownership of a car capable of housing a family of rods, when all I ever wanted was a Mini – and I was paying for the vehicle! How did that happen?

As the discussion continued, we came down the scale to candlelit meals – a bonus point earned if the food is cooked and served by the angler. Take-aways don't count, obviously, although they are granted the basic BP.

Delivery and collection of a spouse/partner to and from a venue on a girls' night out was another little earner, and attending PTA meetings. Bringing in washing on a rainy day constitutes a couple of points, so I was told, especially if it occurred halfway through the big match on TV, and leaving the mobile phone switched on while fishing gets the nod of approval from the non-fishing partner, too.

Someone suggested, jokingly, that holding the foot of a ladder while the wife removes leaves from a gutter, which brought raucous laughter from the group. I didn't tell them that this was a bit too close to home for comfort – the CA was scared of heights so I had to do all the roof work – they wouldn't have believed me, anyway.

The big one after marriage is having the in-laws to stay. Feeding them on a Saturday night is good, but actually moving them in and entertaining them for a week constitutes at least two weekends at a lake. The ultimate sacrifice, though, is agreeing to cancel an anticipated fishing trip in favour of a family event, and to reap the maximum benefit this must be done with an air of serious martyrdom and much muttering under the breath. Care should be taken, though, not to put the negotiation for this one in motion while in the presence of fishing mates. It's far too dangerous to others and could lead to dizzy spells on the part of the onlookers and subsequent visits to A and E. That's a terrible waste of fishing time.

OFF THE HOOK

EPILOGUE

Thirty-four pounds of heaven

I wrote about female anglers with big carp for 15 years, on and off, and never in a million years did I think that one day I'd be writing about myself, and a decent-sized fish in the same sentence! I was totally overwhelmed by my achievement at the time and still get a warm glow when I think about it today.

After the event, I had to apologise to Allan Stone, and to anyone else who was expecting me to turn up at Yateley for the annual Stoney and Friends charity event for the Macmillan Nurses. I was on my way there armed with a shiny new fishing licence in the hope that someone might lend me a rod so I could have a go, but I got side-tracked, big time.

I received a joyful text message in the middle of the night, (as did best part of the Home Counties fishing fraternity), telling me that a friend had achieved a longstanding ambition; he'd caught a 30. I knew what this meant to him so, on my way out the following morning, I grabbed two glasses and a bottle of champagne from my wine rack intending to interrupt his fishing and celebrate for an hour before making my way to Yateley and the charity fish-in.

He was pleased to see me and, over breakfast, offered a blow-by-blow account of his capture. I can tell you now that after a long drive there's nothing better than a huge bacon sarnie and a glass of champers while sitting by a water's edge in early morning sunshine.
"While you're here," he said. "You might as well practise casting. Here, have a go at aiming for that overhanging bush."

Isn't he gorgeous?

After the 257th attempt, okay, it was probably about eight but it felt like a whole lot more, he was satisfied that I'd planted the bait in the right place and then he spotted a friend who had just arrived.

"There's Tex," he said. "I haven't seen him for ages. You don't mind, do you, if I leave you in charge of my rods for ten minutes while I go and have a chat with him? If one of the rods goes just pick it up and turn that little handle."

I did mind, actually. I didn't want to be left with so much responsibility so early in the morning, but I agreed and he wandered off. My friend can talk for England once he gets going so I knew that his 'ten minutes' could develop into half an hour. I made myself comfortable on his bedchair and prepared to enjoy some solitude in glorious surroundings before the onslaught of the day at Yateley.

Minutes after he had left, his right-hand rod screamed off with me screaming behind it. He couldn't hear me; he was well on his way to the other side of the lake and Tex, but I hesitated briefly before picking up the rod and striking, convinced that the absentee would have heard the buzzer and come haring back to the rescue. Not a chance. There was no alternative but to reel in, all the time yelling, in vain, for him to come and get me.

Then, I realised that things were getting serious so I stopped yelling - I had to, really, I was shaking and couldn't breathe for a start - and decided to concentrate, not having a clue what to do. I talked myself calm. Years ago, faced with panicky situations,

I developed this technique, and it still works; maybe, it would be just as effective if applied to the carp. I decided to give it a try. It couldn't do any harm and I was prepared to grovel and beg this creature if necessary, just it to co-operate.

The fish was zig-zagging across the lake and I knew that I had to keep it in the clear bits because there was a considerable amount of weed around and I had no idea where possible snags might be. I was later informed that this fish action is called kiting, it sounds

Gently does it. Still chattin' him up.

like an ancient martial art to me. I began my monologue chat-up line.

"Come on, sweetheart. Just to the left a little bit, there's a good boy. You're doing so well. Don't be frightened. I'm not a proper angler. It's only me, I'll prob'ly never do this again and I won't hurt you. No! No! Not that way. Now you're being silly. Sorry, sorry, I didn't mean it. You're a beautiful fishy, soooo clever and I'm sorry if this is stinging a bit. You've got to come to Mummy, I have to get that nasty hook out for you." Good job my mate was on the other side of the lake, now I come to think of it.

Suddenly the reel locked solid and it was hard to keep hold so I let some line out.

"Oh, okay. Not ready yet? You have a little swim, then," and gently reeled in again. This happened several times and I'm amazed that I had the presence of mind to do what I did. I must have somehow absorbed fishing knowledge from decades of watching others and acted instinctively upon it.

Fifteen minutes later, I could see the fish and between muttering endearments and words of reassurance to him, began yelling again. Clearly, the rod-owner was still deep in conversation, showing off with his tale of personal achievement the night before. What on earth was I going to do, now? I couldn't leave the poor thing swimming round in circles and he'd kill me if I lost it. Somehow or other I had to try and net it.

Now, what would a real carper do? Lay the net in the water adjacent to the fish, then guide it to a convenient angle and slide the net underneath it. That sounded okay in my head. In practise, though, it's not that simple. The fish had a mind of its own and didn't fancy the net at all, despite me telling him that it was 'only a net, you silly boy. I'm sure you've seen a net before. Come on, baby. Let me have you.' Three attempts later and I had him but couldn't lift the net out of the water. More yelling.

Eventually, my cries for help were heeded and a breathless angler came rushing along the path towards me.

"Erm..." I began apologetically; I'd only been there for a short visit, after all. "Erm... I've got this fishy in the net and I can't lift it out."

He muttered something about 'bloody women,' hauled the net from the lake, carried it over to an unhooking mat, and uncovered it. He went very quiet for a moment or two.

"Oh my God," he said. "What have you done?"

I was getting really worried. What had I done? Had I broken it? Killed it? What?

"You've only gone and caught the biggest fish in the lake, you cow! I dunno, leave you alone for five minutes, and you stitch me up."

I began to feel guilty until I realised that he was excited as I was.

"How the hell did you manage to get that in," he said. "Last time that fish was caught it took three anglers and a boat to land it. Stay there and look after the fish. Don't move or touch anything. I'll be back with Gary and a camera." He set off at a power-walk, while I disobeyed and had a deep and meaningful conversation with my beautiful, 34lb mirror carp. I told him how gorgeous he was, that I was going to take the hook out of his mouth and I'd be as gentle as I could.

Minutes later, the real angler returned, followed by the rest of the syndicate members who were all armed with cameras. They'd all arrived to congratulate me and I was impressed with their enthusiasm and friendliness. To a man, they told me how wonderful I was and not one of them sniffed disdainfully because a mere novice, and a female to boot, had caught the fish they'd all been after for months. They are a seriously lovely bevy of blokes.

I have photos of me now. There are few in existence because a prerequisite to having your picture taken, in the circle I mix with is that you must be holding a fish, otherwise, what's the point? So, by the time I'd posed - and, boy, did I pose! - and I'd gone into the water up to thigh level to put my carp back (fully clothed, incidentally. I'd offered to get my kit off but was told emphatically to 'keep 'em on'...you get to a certain age, you know...) it was too late to go to Yateley. Besides which I stank of lake water, was covered in carp juice and had to get home to write it all down and get the photos sorted immediately!

I was completely hooked. I just wanted to do it again, although I was told that it would all be downhill from now on. I'd increased my personal best by about 30 pounds and to top that is nigh on impossible. I didn't care. I just wanted that buzz again. It was half an hour before I stopped shaking.

I had phone calls, text messages promising hugs, beers and other things that I won't mention, and revelled in the glory of it all, until I had a phone call from a mate who had managed to get to Yateley.

"Rosie!" said Elton. "Tim Paisley's just caught a 34.12."

"Noooo! Tell him to put it back and keep quiet. Or kick him in the car-park for me."

"Welcome to the real world of carp fishing," said my tormentor. "The frustration, the elation; the 'someone's caught a bigger one'. You'll have to get over it!"

I got over it. Tim's capture didn't detract one iota from the best weekend I'd had since ....the last best weekend I'd had. I'd caught that carp by accident, after all, but I could understand exactly what drives carp anglers to sit for hours, waiting for days at a time sometimes, for a carp to take a bait. I knew now why some are reluctant to share their secret ingredients, disclose the whereabouts of their venues, all that stuff.

Getting things into perspective and putting my moments of glory aside, though, it was only a carp, for goodness sake. Far more importantly, 15 minutes away from where I was wallowing in adulation from my companions, Stoney and Friends had raised £10,719 for the Macmillan Nurses. What an achievement that was!

So, all you anglers out there who think there's skill attached to capturing and landing a specimen carp, you're wrong. All you need is Sod's Law and a good chat-up line!

How to catch and keep an angler

Ten years ago, in the wake of 'The Guide', I was surprised to receive a response from unattached, prospective fishing widows who told me that they liked the book so much that they wouldn't mind having an angler of their own. Clearly, they believed me when I said that living with anglers could be fun, and much of the time it was. Life was certainly never boring.

I came up with a few ideas to help them in their quest. There are a number of single anglers out there, some of whom have never married but most of them are divorced from women who either had no sense of humour or were unable/unwilling to understand their man's obsession. Maybe it's time someone gave them a good home.

You could spend hours at a water's edge in search of a Realtree clad, and usually taciturn when they're concentrating, unattached angler, but you'd need a dog to walk, as an excuse. Otherwise, you'd look a bit weird and your target would either be very frightened and run away or you'd be arrested for stalking. There are other obvious places to strike up a conversation, though, if you know where to look.

It's no good approaching a carp angler with, "Come on, big boy, show us yer tackle." Many carp anglers show a certain coyness around the human female; note I said 'human', they seem to lose all inhibitions around female carp, or even dogs! There are exceptions, of course. Some of 'em don't know the meaning of the word 'coy', unless it is spelt differently and applied to a variegated patterned species of their chosen prey.

However, for the majority, a far subtler ploy is necessary because men, especially anglers, are hunters at heart and need a challenge. Playing hard to get is vital so you should approach the capture of any angler in the way that they would go after a specimen fish. You will need decent bait. Food and/or sex, tempered with a keen sense of humour are ideal, depending on the age, disposition, and priorities of your quarry, and temptation should be offered with a great deal of guile. Do not present your bait so that it's an obvious enticement.

You could hang about river banks or lake edges at weekend lunchtimes, with dog in tow, or a small child at a pinch, although the latter can sometimes be a deterrent, and await your prey to show itself, but if your fancied angler produces a neatly packed lunch from a clean rucksack, be cautious. Precisely cut sandwiches, yoghurt accompanied by a spoon, and a vacuum flask containing milky tea are dead giveaways, so you must forget him, however attractive; he will have a widow already. On the other hand, if he pulls out a couple of cheese doorsteps, a Pot Noodle and a six-pack you can reckon on a safe bet and begin your operation.

Sea anglers are easier to seduce. They are fun to be with, if you can get over the smell of stale seawater and unspeakable stains on smocks, and when released from a day out, adrift in an open boat, with only 11 other blokes for company, they are rampant and desperate for a feminine wile, or two.

When conversing with an angler of any discipline, express an interest and appear to be impressed by their angling knowledge. Allow them to blind you with their science even though you have read every angling publication you can lay your hands on. Your research will not be wasted. Despite your pretence of ignorance and willingness to be amazed by their expertise, with prior knowledge you will be able to make an intelligent observation or two.

Determine whether your chosen one is of a scientific bent or art inspired. Does talking about the physiological aspects of fish and the chemical reactions within assorted baits turn him on, or does he wax lyrical over nature, wildlife, watercraft, and sunsets? It will be one or the other, trust me.

So, where can you go to meet one of these wonderful men? Obviously anywhere near water, but bear in mind that liquid of any kind, particularly beer, seems to attract them and they gravitate towards it. Sea anglers, in particular, tend to congregate for an hour or two in the harbour pub after a fishing trip, in order to 'action re-play' the day's events on the high seas. They seem unable to pass a saloon bar door without having at least a couple of pints, either to celebrate a good catch or to drown their sorrows after a fishless expedition.

A word of warning, here: don't bother waiting near wharves at low tide. You'll be wasting your time because they won't return until there's enough depth to manoeuvre the boat up to the landing stage and you'll be far better off waiting, fragrant and attractive, in the bar. Spotting a posse of sea-anglers is quite easy. They have strange sartorial habits, for a start, and these vary from Captain Birdseye oilskins, thigh-high waders folded down so that they look like wellies, and ancient smocks, to T-shirts, and stiff jeans from accumulated rag-worm and soft-crab juices. There will always be a whiff of squid or stale seawater emanating from their clothes, varying from mild to downright offensive, depending on how much time they have put in and how warm it is in the snug.

Initially, they will be discussing the day's play and will focus on the ones that got away, but if you are patient, and wait until they've consumed a couple of pints, their concentration will lapse, they begin to notice their surroundings and you may receive a smile or even the offer of half a shandy.

Only venture toward a lake or river if you are prepared to sit out long sessions, in all weathers, biding your time until they consider offering attention to anything, or anyone, out of the water. Practise the art of making your eyelashes flicker, to look like a lure, i.e. a plastic, fish-shaped gizmo or a metal rotating spoon affair, both of which flutter through water to attract fish. You could even pluck your eyebrows into the shape of dorsal fins if you're really keen, and try opening and shutting your mouth a lot; nothing gets an angler going like a good pout.

Don't hang around near wharves...

Camping accessory shops are good places, too. Look for men buying camping stoves or replacement gas canisters. They are usually dressed for fishing because they leave everything until the last minute and will be making their purchases on the way to a venue.

So, early mornings in tackle shops or late evenings in pubs should enable you to spot one, and then there's always the supermarket. Look for men who fill a trolley with TV dinners for themselves, and do not be discouraged if the dinners are marked 'feeds two'; the average size of a 'feeds one' pack would not satisfy a five-year-old. If they add tins of sweetcorn, Spam, chickpeas, beans, cake flavourings, bottles of food colouring and dog biscuits to their shopping, they are single anglers, believe me.

As far as clothing goes, you should stick to nature's colours; grey, green, brown, camo gear, and for maximum impact, if things get really desperate, I always found that rubber or waxed cotton goes down well. Make sure that you have plenty of zips dotted around your clothing, too. Anglers seem to enjoy playing with the zips on rod bags and assorted luggage and sometimes will develop a compulsion to unzip anything at all.

So, let's assume that you've caught one. How do you manage to keep hold of your mate? I'll tell you a secret: if you tolerate their foibles, many and various, join in, to a point, with preparation, running errands and so on, most of them will appreciate your efforts and harmony will reign. Make time to be with them when they are not fishing; there will be plenty of angler-free hours when you can do the things that you want to do when they are out for hours, sometimes days, at a stretch. Rearrange your own schedule to coincide with their rare spells at home. Time is a man-made dimension and open to flexibility.

Once caught, nurtured, and treated with respect, an angler makes an ideal partner. One day, you might even want to go fishing yourself.

The next generation

The last thing I want is to bore other people with stories of my family and particularly my grandchildren. Don't you hate that, when grandparents insist on telling you the latest anecdote or the cute things that their grandchildren have uttered? I am guilty of it myself, but I only tell those who I consider to be close friends because I know they'll indulge me - and besides, I have to listen to them doing it; it's only fair!

Our little ones cannot be ignored, though. They will all be fascinated by water, as were their fathers, it's in their genes and the budding obsession is already being actively encouraged by both sets of parents.

It all started with Lucy. She and Simon have been together now for over a decade and in a couple of years, she will be a fully-fledged angling mum, without doubt. Simon goes sea fishing with his brother, carp/pike fishing whenever he can and his little boys, Thomas and William, clamour to go to the seaside at every opportunity, in all weathers. Fortunately, they live near the coast, so the requests are met, and it's no sacrifice, because Simon and Lucy enjoy being near water, too.

Anyway, back to the plot. One Monday morning, when Simon and his then new-ish girlfriend, Lucy, were on their first holiday together, I received a phone call.
"I'm in Cumbria, Ma," he said, "the drugs capital of the world – or is that Colombia? Anyway, I'm in the Lake District and I can't find anywhere to fish."
I suggested that he look out of the car window.
"You're surrounded by water," I said. "There must be something, somewhere, swimming about that'll give itself up."

I was only kidding. I did know that day-ticket, carp-fishing waters in that part of the country weren't quite as abundant as down south. There are more of them now, I believe, but ten years ago, they were a bit thin on the ground.

I suggested that they have a go for other species but they were not what Simon was after. It was Monday; they only had another six days and time was a-wasting, so he demanded that I use all my resources to find him somewhere to go and to ring him back as soon as possible. His mobile phone battery was down to one bar and desperation was creeping into his voice.

I had a look on the Internet. Anglers Net has always had a comprehensive list of fisheries all over Britain, with phone numbers and addresses, so I did a quick ten-minute research, wrote everything down and phoned him. It wasn't good news. "There are a few day-ticket coarse fisheries that contain carp," I said, "but if I were you, I'd head toward North Wales. They're more into the kind of fishing you want to do, and I know that your brother had a fantastic week carp fishing there."

The phone went quiet and I worried that they were wandering around lost, but a couple of days later, there was another call to let me know that they were okay. They were camped by a lake near Beaumaris, Anglesey. Simon had given up on me as a source of inspiration and wisely telephoned his big brother for advice, which is what he should have done in the first place.

When I said I wanted a bucket and spade...

"You'll never guess what!" said my clearly jubilant offspring, but pretending to be gutted because his girlfriend was listening.

"Dopey's only gone and caught a carp!" Dopey, aka Lucy Wright, is far from it. She's an intelligent beauty and has the necessary, dare I say vital, sense of humour to be a companion to Simon. When they first met, we assumed that her surname was the primary reason for them getting together in the first place, because he's been looking for Miss Right ever since he was old enough to - er - vote. We soon became aware of Lucy's qualities, though.

"It was only a four-pounder," he went on, "but it's bigger than anything I've had here, so far. We'll tell you all about it when we get back."

It turned out that while fishing on the first day, Lucy had picked up Simon's other rod, which had

screamed off while he was dealing with a small carp.
She lost the fish, as did he incidentally, but had felt
the thrill of the chase and wanted to join in.

There was an Argos store in a nearby town so Simon
bought a basic £15.99 kid's kit and a fishing licence
for her. I asked him why the necessity to purchase a
'plastic' fishing outfit when he had two perfectly
good rods at the lakeside already. Hadn't I taught my
sons to share?

"I'm not having her touch any of my gear," he cried,
indignantly. "You mad, or what?"

Lucy had a wonderful fishing holiday, she told me
later, apart from a couple of incidents that made her
retire to the bivvy and hide.
"I was sitting there, Rosie, really happy and content.
We had just eaten so Simon was in a good mood and
everything was really lovely. I happened to look
down at my left leg and noticed all this white stuff
oozing from under my trousers. It really scared me,
I thought I'd picked up some terrible lakeside
disease like leprosy, or something."
Not Lucy's best subject at the time, medical
knowledge; she's practically an expert now, having
had two babies and nursed them through all manner
of horrible ailments.

She went on. "Anyway, I pulled up my trouser leg
and there was a slug. What scared me was, I hadn't
felt it go up there. I must have been so caught up in
the atmosphere of the lake that I just didn't feel

anything and there could have been all kinds of creepy-crawlies all over me, for all I knew. The slug was hideous; all white with a green stripe down it's back. I plucked it off, threw it as far as I could, and then just had to find a shower, pronto. Simon went mad! What do you think he said?"

I knew perfectly well, what he would have said. He'd have thought the disposal of a slug to be a terrible waste when he could have shoved it on a hook and tempted a carp with it. I lost count of the number of times I prevented him, and his brother, from experimenting to the detriment of newborn frogs and other innocent wriggling things at a water's edge.

"And then there was the bat," Lucy continued. "It kept whizzing round my head, and I had my hair down. It kept swooshing toward my hair and I had to get into the bivvy for protection until it went away." We tried to tell her that bats have a built-in radar system and the last thing it would have enjoyed was to be tangled to death in Lucy's hair, but she wouldn't bow to our superior knowledge. "It was going to nest in my hair and raise a family of baby bats," she insisted. We left it.

Lucy soon overcame her distaste for potential baits and managed to put her own maggots on a hook, tie rigs, play with foul-smelling boilies and was generally shaping up to be a proper angler, acquiring her fishing knowledge from Simon and from her own mistakes. She's going to need all the help she can get soon. As I write this Thomas is four and William two years old. Give it a couple of years and she'll be out there in all weathers with a packed lunch and a box of maggots or rag worm. I speak from experience.

Have you got one, Mum? Let's have a go!

One fishing widow/mum down, one to go; and then there was our lovely Kate. She had only known number one son for just over six months when he had to go to Mexico to take part in a World Wide Fishing Safari, in a tournament. When Kate suggested that she go with him, he was quick to point out that this was a work-related trip and it wasn't going to be all fun and games. Kate booked herself a ticket, anyway; she might as well get used to it, she reasoned, seeing as the man in her life seemed to be obsessed with swimming things and that wasn't about to change.

They were out on a boat in Cabo St Lucas, and Kate was happy just to watch, mainly because it was a competition but more to the point, she'd never touched a rod in her life before and maybe game fish were not the best species to practise on. Apparently, it was only billfish that counted in this particular tournament; marlin, sailfish - only fish with a beak. Like I said, Kate was only there for the ride and the occasional beer, enjoying the sun in shorts and a T-shirt while showing a keen interest on all that was going on around her.

Soon there was a take on Dave's rod and he called out as he moved away from the chair at the back of the boat.
"Come on, Kate! It's a dorado. That doesn't count for anything, no points involved at all. Jump in, it's only a dorado. You can practise on this."
Kate jumped into the chair as directed and as she grabbed the rod there was a huge explosion of water.
"Er...do you want this back now? I think a bigger fishy has eaten the dorado."
She was right. A 200lb striped marlin had, indeed, eaten the dorado – line, hook, livebait and all.
"No, it's your fish," Dave replied. "You've touched the rod so you've got to get it in now; that's the rules." Dave was secretly gutted but pleased, in a way, that it was Kate who'd got the fish on, and not one of the others aboard.
"Oh no! Are you sure you don't want this? I haven't a clue what to do!" Kate tried to hand it over, but the boyfriend wasn't having any of it.
"Don't worry, I'll talk you through it," he said.

"It took an hour to reel in," Kate told me after the event. "It felt like taking a rhino for a walk with

My arms hurt!

Dave giving instructions all the time. 'Let the line out, wind it in,' over and over again. I got it nearly to the boat, and it whizzed off again. Then it went under the boat and down for miles."

"Let it wear itself out," was the best advice the expert could offer.

"That was all very well," said Kate, "but it was so strong, I could imagine it taking days before it was worn out! Every time, just when I thought I'd got it in, it would tear off again and my arms felt like they were about to drop off. After a while, though, adrenalin started to kick in, which helped, plus I have a stubborn nature so I was determined to get it. I felt no pain but I was shaking like a leaf, and all Dave kept saying was 'let it tire itself out'. What about me? It was a case of who would tire out the fastest!

"I don't know how many times I wound in and let out line, but bit by bit, I managed to get it closer and closer to the boat until I could catch a glimpse of it and I can remember saying 'Wow! That's massive' - and then, after about an hour in stupidly hot, 100 degree heat, I finally got it in."

Kate made the mistake of giving it a cuddle and ended up covered in slime and what looked like red ant bites that itched like mad. The fish was weighed and put back into the water while its captor put cream on her wounds.

"Still, I did yank it out of it's home, so I didn't blame it for burning me a little bit," said Kate, "and everyone wanted to buy me beer. By that time, my arms had locked up. I've been going to the gym for years but nothing prepares you for using the fishing muscles. That first beer was the best I'd ever had, even though I couldn't move my arms so Dave had to get me a straw. He was so proud of me that day, he told everyone. 'Guess what she got! Only the biggest marlin caught this month!' All the other fish caught that day were around 90 to 120lbs. There were a couple that weighed in at 140lbs but mine was 200lbs! It was a fantastic experience!"

Another fantastic experience was their honeymoon in Kenya. They spent every other day out fishing and stayed in a hotel that specialised in fishing holidays. Kate caught five sailfish, a king fish, and a dorado. "I was reeling stuff in all the time," she said, "it was amazing."

The best honeymoon present ever!

Kate has thrown herself into fishing widowhood with a vengeance, although I don't think she's quite got the hang of it yet. At eight months pregnant, she tagged along on a beach fishing trip to Cromer, in the middle of November.

"I sat there for hours," said Kate, "in the pitch black, with just a little camping light on top of the rod. Dave cooked us a can of Stag, lava-hot chilli each, washed down with equally hot coffee, but I was still freezing. It's quite hard to get warm clothes to fit in late pregnancy, and it's a good thing that I didn't care what I looked like. I was decked out in an enormous set of, dry-suit dungarees and a huge jacket but I wasn't wearing enough layers for proper insulation. I'd been perched on a tiny stool, for hours and hours, began to have stomach cramps and began to get scared that I would have our first baby on the beach. I had no idea what labour was supposed to feel like; I was in agony.

"It turned out to be indigestion and quite a lot of trapped wind. Dave packed up as fast as he could, as I rushed towards the car, bent over double. Because I thought I'd gone into labour, Dave drove really quickly and once at the house I told him that the bag for the hospital was packed, but first I needed to go to the toilet. Well, to put it politely, everything fell out except the baby and I had to say, "Oops, sorry, Dave. I seem to be okay now. I'm not having the baby, actually, I just needed a poo."

At their wedding, during the groom's speech, Dave told of the moment he knew she was the one for him. "I thought, 'she can't cook, can't clean, can't iron...but she's gorgeous and she can catch a marlin; she's a keeper!'"

Dave and Kate have two little girls, Mia (three) and Holly (six months) and they will be subjected to the fishing scene, too. Dave's been an editor of sea-fishing magazines nearly all his working life and chases carp and chub in his limited spare time, so angling is in his blood. When he found out he was going to have a daughter, did he put her name down immediately for Roedean? Er...no. A custom-made, pink, half-size fishing rod was his priority. Mia loves it and already holds the rod correctly and casts far better than I ever did, and probably her mum by now. It's a bit early to suss out how Holly will react to the inevitability of fishing in her life, but we all know she won't have much choice in the matter.

Every angler should make the effort to take their kids fishing, if they want to join in. I have known those, over the years, who refused to do so because their offspring got in the way and reduced their own pleasure, but the advantages to be gained by the younger generation should override all that because kids can learn so much, without realising it.

Apart from the obvious benefit of being outdoors and not stuck inside with a computer game, they learn life skills; how their actions affect others, how effort equals reward and how to interact with others. Self-discipline – sadly lacking in today's society, I fear – is another vital lesson learned while angling, and there are many more. I reckon it should be included in the national curriculum.

They've got to start somewhere.

Come on, Daddy! The fishes are waiting.

THE FRENCH
CONNECTION

Farm, Frog and French things

For years, I'd been used to being a kind of hanger-on, my presence on fishing trips tolerated for the services I could offer, i.e. preparing food, going to a nearby tackle shop for forgotten items, driving my angler(s) to a chosen venue, and other non-fishing duties. I knew my place in the pecking order and was quite happy to be there, most of the time.

There were occasions, though, when I became bored, cold, windswept, and/or tired but couldn't leave because I had wait until the CA was ready to go back home. So, if anyone had ventured to suggest that, one day, I'd camp out in France, on my own, with a load of carp anglers and enjoy it immensely, I'd have laughed at them. However, that's exactly what happened and a whole week spent in the company of friends and French carp sped by unbelievably quickly - so quickly, in fact, that I felt I'd only been away for a few days and didn't want to come home.

We arrived at Farm Lake after a smooth ferry crossing, and a two-hour coach journey travelling through picturesque and historic France. Is it just me, or do others feel an atmosphere of sadness and stillness in Picardy? I felt it even before roadside signs informed me that we were travelling through the area of the Somme. It took me a while to shake off the feeling of wretchedness and to get my brain back to the matter in hand, but maybe I'm just over-sensitive.

My priority on arrival, of course, was to suss out the facilities. To my deep joy, I discovered proper loos and showers. Who could ask for more? Oh, yes, the fishing. Of course, I knew there was something.

We spent two nights at Farm Lake where two of our party caught a brace of 30s between them, before moving on to Frog Lake, a few miles away, for a further four nights. We were one swim short at Frog so I was unable to fish but despite that being the main reason for my visit, it didn't seem to matter. I was quite happy watching the others, enjoying their triumphs, sympathising with small disasters, cooking meals, and generally getting in the way.

The weather wasn't too bad; it was warm enough to lie in the sun during the day but absolutely freezing at night. For one who isn't used to sleeping on a bed chair in the middle of nowhere, this was quite an experience. I still haven't acquired the knack of getting back into a sleeping bag after a midnight visit to the bushes and I've reached the age when that cannot be avoided. Every single night my borrowed bed collapsed under me and I shivered as I tried to reinstate it, all the time worrying in case, this time, I had managed to break it beyond repair and would have to confess to the owner. All part of life's rich tapestry, so I was told, unsympathetically by the angler who fixed it for me eventually with a couple of bungee straps.

A week previously, the gamekeeper had shot a wild boar which, he reckoned, weighed in at 500 kilos but my companions didn't tell me that until after we had returned home. I thought it considerate of them. You can bet your life that the boar would have had a friend or two. Prior knowledge could have severely curtailed my nocturnal bathroom visits, caused all kinds of kidney trouble and I don't know who would have been more startled in confrontation, a boar, or me.

I mustn't leave out the only downside event that could have marred the whole week for me. I very rarely get into a strop about anything, I'm too lazy and few things in life are worth the energy expended in losing one's temper, but they made me go shopping. I absolutely hate it under any circumstances. It's such a waste of precious time, forces me into crowds, and causes stress at the best of times. On this occasion, I worried because I imagined I might have bought something the others wouldn't like (and I was spending their money) besides which, everything was priced in euros and currency conversion while thinking on my feet is not my strongest point.

I wandered round the French equivalent of Sainsbury, anxious and fed-up, bought what I thought would be enough to knock up into meals for the week so I didn't have to repeat the misery, and arrived back at the lake hot, tired, hungry, and very cross. I should have known that the lads couldn't have cared less what I'd spent their cash on as long as they were fed and watered, but I made sure I avoided everyone for an hour until I'd calmed down, and then comforted myself by cooking a meal. They all made the right noises but I wasn't sure if they really meant it, or if they were trying to avert another sulk. We all retired replete and happy, anyway.

Frog Lake is very pretty if a tad noisy. We were fairly close to a motorway and during the night, mad French truckers - clearly carp anglers, themselves - hooted their horns in camaraderie. What with the flight path to Orly airport and manic geese on patrol I wondered if I would get any sleep at all, but it's odd how quickly one becomes accustomed to things and by the second night I didn't notice the racket.

I just love cooking for a horde.

To add to the noise, buzzers were going off all night and my neighbouring angler was out of his sleeping bag and running supportively whenever anyone else's bite alarms screamed. By the end of the week, though, a general air of complacency had set in so when his rod screamed off in the wee, small, freezing hours, no one arrived to offer assistance.

"You all right?" I yelled from my nice warm cocoon.
"Yep. All under control. Go back to sleep," was the response.
Was he having a laugh, or what? I'm not kidding; the noise was unbelievable. Apart from the forte/allegro movement by the Delkim Symphony Orchestra, as all three rods bleeped alarmingly with an almost reggae rhythm, and the squawking chorus of rudely-awakened wildlife, our hero was cursing fortissimo because the fish had snagged his middle rod and yet there was not a sign of a fellow angler to lend assistance. I wouldn't have been surprised to hear reports of a couple of French graveyards in the vicinity showing signs of disturbance, the noise was so great.

Eventually, unable to bear my mate's suffering (and the noise) any further, I hauled myself out of bed. It took a few minutes because I couldn't find my jeans in the dark and there was certainly no time to find shoes. So there I stood, holding by turns, landing net, rod, and carp sack, barefoot in the park, rapidly turning into the ice maiden and losing the will to live. Was it worth it? Oh, yes. He caught a 30 and started to sing; as if he hadn't made enough commotion for one night!

In between the catching of glorious carp and entertaining evening socials round a Coleman, or two,

I listened to the technical discussions taking place both pre and post catch.

"These are French carp under English pressure," said our bailiff, Olivier. "Eight months of the year they are fished constantly and, as a result, are wary and easily spooked."

Oh yeah? Is that right? Given the volume of bankside cabaret, they didn't appear to be particularly nervous to me.

My companions went on, and on, about hook links, running rigs, carp possibly freaking at the sight of a PVA bag, the necessity for small handfuls of bait, half a dozen crumbed-up boilies and a few pellets around the hook bait - and on. All of which meant little to me but these beautiful carp, scared or not, were worth waiting for. Magnificent, bright, shiny

Magnificent, bright shiny creature, and the fish isn't bad, either!

creatures were brought forth from clear water to be admired, photographed, and returned with as much deference as they deserved; truly magical.

One morning there was a discussion about a coypu that had been found dead on the edge of one of the swims. It was huge and marvellous and we were trying to tell our French bailiff about it.

"Muskrats do grow to a fair size," said one angler.

To clarify matters for our bailiff's benefit, another of our party said, "that's coypu" in case the Frenchman didn't know what a muskrat was.

"No, honestly. He's telling the truth," said Terry, razor-sharp, as ever, to spot a pun. Koi poo, or carp s*** in case you don't get it. The bailiff didn't and his face was a picture as he tried to work it out...you had to be there really. We tried not to allow hysteria to take us over but it's so hard when you know that you shouldn't laugh too much for fear of causing offence. The bailiff looked worried. I'm sure he must have thought we were either taking the mickey or verging on insanity.

I had a wonderful time chilling out, talking to friends, laughing, and cooking; it was my idea of heaven. There was an unfortunate incident during one of the 'cooking for a multitude' exercises. Trying to balance a wok on a single burner while adding a splash of red wine to enhance flavours needs three hands, I discovered. Our supper went everywhere, all over the path, and as there was only just enough to go round in the first place, it couldn't possibly be wasted. So during the stunned silence and in full view of my prospective diners, I scooped up the big bits and bunged it back into the wok. Heated through to furnace temperature it would be okay to eat. I made sure that any bacteria would be thoroughly sterilised before I served it up. I've often wondered what it would be like to eat grits, now I know. All credit to my companions, though; they ate every scrap. There's loyalty for you!

I have to thank my partners in crime for a wonderful week. Dave, Jimmers, Tel, Tony, and Colin made it special. Colin kept me supplied with chocolate, at considerable risk to himself, I have to say. Not many would have had the courage to tap on my bivvy after I had retired to hand me a packet of M&Ms and a Bounty! My sons, David and Simon, deserved a round of applause, too. They took turns and gave up their respective Saturday nights to drive long distances in order to ensure the safe delivery and collection of their mother to and from Folkestone.

Oops! Waste not, want not.

A party of happy anglers arrived back

in Blighty after an exhausting week. I needed a hot, frothy bath and a facial, but the boys were all relaxed and beaming. They'd caught fish. Nothing else seemed to matter much.

Reach for the Sky

Following the success of the Frog and Farm adventure, I went with a different set of lads to Sky Lake for a week. It's near Meaux - pronounced Mo but referred to as Mucks by my companions who read French phonetically and whose limited vocabulary includes phrases picked up from Del-boy on Only Fools and Horses; 'bonnet de douche,' 'garçon, les petits pois,' and 'may we, may we' being the most popular.

We arrived late morning, wearing T-shirts and jeans in warm spring sunshine, and as we unpacked a mountain of gear from the minibus and started to assemble it all, I realised just how much I had been nurtured and cherished by my angling mates over the past decade. I'd never had to put up a bivvy on my own, and had just taken it for granted that the lads I happened to be with just hauled it into position without any preamble or effort. It's not as easy as it looks, I discovered.

First, you have to discover the direction of prevailing winds, make sure that the rods can be seen from the door while holding a can of something and lying supine on a bedchair, and then caress the groundsheet carefully, to look for any stones or tree roots that may be underneath. These could damage knees while kneeling inside the bivvy, they told me; do they pray to the carp gods? I didn't ask. Then, there's the putting in of pegs round the outside, mathematically and securely placed, ensuring that the groundsheet is on top of the bivvy perimeter material and rolling up the front door with military precision so that it looks pretty. Just watching all this wore me out; I was exhausted by the time I had a home to go to, but not ungrateful.

Sky is 15 acres of totally tree-lined lake and boasted of carp up to and beyond 50lbs. So, having set up, we cooked a decent supper, imbibed a couple of bottles of local plonk and fell into sleeping bags, secure in the knowledge that the following week would be idyllic; no phones, no crowds, good fishing and warmish weather.

We awoke to a sharp frost and a biting easterly wind. From then onward, the weather nose-dived into hail the size of small marbles, frost by midnight, and that east wind was relentless. There were remarkably clean loos, though, and hot showers in the clubhouse where I was allowed into the kitchen to cook a decent fry-up every morning.

At one point, there was a criticism from one of the party sitting around the tables, hands poised over eating irons and eagerly awaiting sustenance that I had forgotten to cook the mushrooms. "You can't cook mushrooms," I said with a superior air, "until the fat has been released from the bacon, unless you want

Is nothing sacred? They even snapped me on my way to the loo!

your breakfast swimming in oil, that is." It went very quiet after that.

To quote Billy Connolly 'There is no such thing as bad weather - just the wrong clothes!' Unfortunately, I had taken literally the advice offered by my fellow anglers who had assured me that during the preceding week in Meaux, it had been warm during the day with just a slight nip in the air at night. I had packed jeans, a couple of light sweaters and one fleece. My companions who were far more experienced than me in spending time at a water's edge, had catered for all temperatures and proceeded to donate various items of clothing to the poor widow-woman in their midst. I borrowed over-trousers from one, socks from another, a kind of kamikaze hat, gloves, sweaters, and a thermal fleece. I have hidden the photos.

Despite the cold, the carp seemed to be quite keen for Carp Company baits and the excitement that had begun with the capture of a fine, 20-pound common the night before by one of our party, continued in the form of a 33-pound mirror which, as the rod screamed off, was offered to me. I'm ashamed to admit that I chickened out, not feeling confident enough to bring it in. Although I had landed a 34lb mirror back in England, I had no idea how big this fish might be and it could have been a 50, for goodness sake. The 34 had taken me 20 minutes of sheer panic and had drained my chatting up reserves for a month afterwards so I didn't want to take the risk. I did hold it, though, and spoke to it gently while they were faffing about with cameras.

Just a small observation on the landing of large carp - well, any carp, really. I wondered aloud why it took three of them to arrange it on an unhooking mat. They seemed to be making an unnecessary song and dance about it. I was told that the fish was a large one, so obviously it took three people; did I know nothing? They had to make sure fins were facing the right way and not in danger of being squashed under its weight; they said the water poured over its gills was not to make it look shiny and cool in the photo at all, but to keep the gills wet and the fish calm. One angler held the carp securely, another put antiseptic on any wounds, and a third held a wet cloth over the fish's head while all this was going on. Only when they were satisfied that they had done all they could for the carp was I allowed to hold it up for a photo.

My instruction continued. I was taught how to catapult boilies into the lake toward a marker some

They let me hold it.

yards away. First with a throwing stick, which they told me to substitute for a catapult because I was a danger to myself and those around me, but the catty caused me considerable pain because I wasn't doing it properly. After persevering for a good half an hour, I was left with a bruise, the size of a 50p piece, at the base of my thumb, but I managed to hit the target eventually to my own satisfaction and so could give up on catapulting and progress to the next stage of my instruction, sweeping the bottom of the lake.

What a fuss! I wasn't that bad at chucking!

Sitting in Rick Golder's bivvy, for a 30-minute respite, a cuppa and a gossip, I complained about the bruised thumb and the fact that my hands were becoming like autumn leaves due to peeling potatoes, for their supper, in icy cold water, in conditions reminiscent of the North Pole. Rick sympathised greatly, probably because he had not been fed since breakfast, and offered me some of his Vaseline Intensive Care hand cream to ease my discomfort. I accepted gratefully.

Later, one of the others pointed out chafed skin on his own hands and innocently, I promise you, I recommended Rick's hand cream. They wouldn't leave the poor boy alone after that. All week he suffered remarks questioning his masculinity and his fellow anglers even suggested renaming the lake if his penchant for hand cream became common knowledge back home. "They'll have to call this sKY lake," they said, making particular reference to some kind of jelly. Rick accused me of grassing him up and was known as Vaz for the rest of the week.

So, this sweeping a rod from side to side in an attempt to discover features on the lakebed, then; I had no idea it could be so revealing and found it fascinating to imagine what might be under the surface, although my imagination was made redundant as my instructor told me what the features might be. If the lead travels fairly smoothly, then it's probably silt; if the rod vibrates then you're over gravel and carp sometimes clean bits of the lake bottom by feeding intensively in one spot. If the rod judders and jerks then it'll more than likely be weed (rigid hornwort, would you believe I was even told the variety!) and if it stops suddenly there'll be a snag.

I was also shown how to measure the depth of two or three spots along the same sweeping line. This was in order to establish such things as ledges, gravel-bars and beds of lilies under the water. These features, I was told, are more often than not, where fish feed. I understand that all this might seem a bit obvious and possibly mundane to you proper carpers but, like the bacon fat/mushroom cooking logic which is second nature to me because I've cooked a squillion fried breakfasts, this angling enlightenment was a necessary ingredient toward any future expertise I might acquire.

Halfway through the week, Terry was over the moon to land a 30lb mirror caught on a zig-rig with an 8-foot hook link in 12 feet of water at 120 yards range, a seemingly impossible idea. However, Tel is capable of the big chuck and managed to reach the distant spot, miraculously without ianything tangling. They were all muttering something about feathering but I was too embarrassed to show ignorance and ask; one of these days I'll find out what it all means.

Wadey moved three times to achieve his haul and spent much of his time in the teeth of a gale, at one point having to hang on to his brolly for dear life. Walking to his swim to deliver a cup of coffee was like going from the Bahamas into Siberia. I was warm as toast compared to him, and while I was tucked up in some of his clothing, he shivered in an east wind that blew round his …er…boilies.

Rick, who had attained a considerable reputation for leaving everything to the last minute, (probably, too engrossed in making sure his hands were nice and soft) screamed off with just hours to spare before we were due to leave. With gritted teeth, he battled a 35-pounder, his shiny, new pride-and-joy rod bent double. He was, I was told, flat-rodded a couple of times, although I didn't know what that meant, either, at the time, and thoroughly deserved his prize. It was a beautiful carp and much adulation was offered to both fish and captor; they still called him Vaz, though.

So, during a bad weather week, a total of ten fine carp were caught to three anglers. Not a bad result, all things considered; and speaking of results, I just have to tell you that my worst fears regarding the acquisition of groceries were not realised. As mentioned previously, I have a real retail phobia and I'll do practically anything to avoid shopping. I was dreading it and yes, I am fully aware that it is weird for a woman to feel like this. However, I went reluctantly and only because he

Soft hands pay off, evidently. Rick Golder with his 35lb mirror.

promised to have the heating on at full blast in the van, with Wadey. I warned him in advance not to take any notice if I was crabby on the way back, that it was nothing personal but just my extreme reaction to any kind of shopping and I'd get over it within an hour or two, providing I was left alone.

Wadey turned out to be my hero. We entered the Supermarket, bought wine, chocolate, bread, meat, fresh vegetables – note the order of priority - paid up and left in a total of 20 minutes, tops. I was so impressed with this that, a couple of days later, when Wadey asked me if I'd care to go with him to get a phone charger, and more chocolate and wine as one or the other of us had overindulged ourselves, I jumped at the chance. At least I'd be warm in the van; the weather was still freezing.

I experienced the same scenario, same brief encounter. Brilliant!

Predictably, the day of our return to Blighty dawned bright, sunny, warm, and a week later, I found out that the boys who ran the lake had developed a tan! It was fun, though. We spent best part of the week laughing at our meteorological misfortune and my companions caught enormous carp so we were happy enough, just cold. Next time I go to France, though, I'll pack a hot water bottle and a duvet or two as a precaution.

Busy doing nothing

The last French trip for carp that I went on was pure indulgence for me. I had no intention of fishing. I'd been asked to go along to write a piece about the venue we visited and I intended to do just that, and nothing else. I'd been told that there wasn't even any cooking for me to do, which I found quite a novelty, to begin with, since that had never happened before, on any fishing expedition I'd been on.

First impressions were of flowers and warmth not only due to the 90-degree heat but also to genuine hospitality. Adjacent to the clubhouse there was a huge oak, sporting squillions of acorns, and a hazel tree laden with nuts and bright-red gladioli, busy-lizzies in pots, blooming shrubs, and undulating lawns that swept down to the lakeside completed the picture. I was looking forward to a week of uncharacteristic inactivity and getting stuck into reading a couple of books while lazing in the sun.

Carp were topping, throwing themselves out of the water in displays of 'come on then, if you think you're hard enough', so things looked promising for my companions, but the whole point of me being there, I was told, was to be completely idle. I lasted until the Tuesday until the compulsion to cook something and then wash up just would not be denied and I had to beg access to the kitchen for an hour or two; they let me bake an apple pie.

We sat up late every night, gossiping and listening to the frog chorus, hedgehogs rootling, coypu and water rats scuttling…how frogs so small can overwhelm collective birdsong and a wedding party in the local village hall is one of the mysteries of nature. I looked forward to their orchestral manoeuvres in the dark. It was like being sung to sleep; not that I know what that's like.

One afternoon, in searing heat, I was taken to a supermarket by the proprietor of the lake, where I bought a barrow load of snacks. We were provided with a huge full English every morning and an even bigger evening meal but lads get peckish about 3pm and since I was the only one not fishing, I'd been detailed to prevent the hunger pangs. On the way back, we had a couple of beers in a local bar and my host then ordered a BMW, which he told me I had to try as it was a 'local speciality'. I found out afterwards that it was more local to London than Paris and comprised one shot of Baileys, one of Malibu and two - count 'em - two of whisky.

I fell for it because I know very little about alcoholic drinks. I know a bit about wine and I'll have a couple of glasses with a meal, but that's about my limit, mainly because I hate not being in control of my brain. However, by the time we arrived back at the lake, the alcohol had kicked in. To the disgust of some - including me - and the amusement of others of our party, I demolished a fishing chair as I tried to sit down, fell over in the shower, and broke a plastic coat hanger while trying to force a dress over my head, without first removing it. I spilt a pint of Diet Coke down the front of a brand new cotton dress and then, several hours later, threw up. I put it down to the weather and had an early night. The weather was far too hot to talk, anyway, although the frogs didn't think so.

Busy doing nothing!

On the last night, we sat, chatting until after midnight, watching the water and counting the species of wildlife we'd seen over the week, anticipating a sleepless night during which carp would be queuing up to be unhooked and lovingly replaced into a heaving habitat. That didn't happen but I'd had a fabulous week doing absolutely sod all, apart from scribbling a few hundred words. That's my kind of fishing holiday!

OFF THE HOOK

LAST WORD

I acquired a new mobile phone recently and spent an afternoon transferring numbers manually. Why the software transferred some contacts automatically from my old mobile, and ignored others, I have no idea. No doubt there is a logical, bloke solution to the problem, but I don't need to know. I've done it now and I don't care. I can hear you thinking, 'for God's sake, woman, get to the point', so I will. While I was ploughing my way through about 300 numbers, I noticed that 95% of my contacts are anglers, anglers' partners or those who work in angling in some capacity. It's hardly surprising really, I've been around those who fish for most of my adult life so there were bound to have been a few! I was surprised that the percentage was so high, though.

Being surrounded by so many fishy folk has been a distinct advantage over the years. It has enabled me to get to know many of them, to call quite a few of them friends and given me the opportunity to work within the fishing media with some of the top names in carp, coarse and sea angling. Never in my wildest dreams would I have imagined I'd be doing that.

It's a standing joke among my angling friends that I once landed a carp by mistake, and I shouldn't take any credit for it at all, really; the angler whose rod I was looking after had done all the hard work, all I did was chat it up and reel it in. It was still exciting, though, and gave me an insight into why anglers go fishing in all weathers and conditions. Everything is done for a reason, or so they say, and that experience allowed me to understand aspects of the sport that I wouldn't otherwise have done.

The real captures, though, are in my specimen album. They are the anglers who I've met along the way and although there are a couple that I've either thrown back or allowed to escape, I'm very lucky to have retained most of them as friends. Long may it continue!

OFF THE HOOK

APPENDIX

I've included this piece, which was written when the eldest was going through a difficult time; he had been made redundant, had no prospects, very few qualifications, and no direction. Tim Paisley published Dave's first professional piece of writing in Carpworld, and with too few GCSEs under his belt, but on the strength of that article, number one son gained admittance to a media studies course, and hasn't looked back. Tim was, indirectly, the starting point for Dave's career as an angling editor. Thanks, Tim. We owe you.

The Quest, by Dave Barham
Previously Published in Carpworld April 1994

An unexpected experience six years ago triggered off my interest in fishing for carp. While float fishing my local club water for perch, I accidentally hooked and landed the lake's biggest fish at that time; a 25½lb mirror carp.

My birthday had just passed and my father had given me a 13ft, carbon match rod, and a Browning graphite reel. This was fairly high-tech gear to me in those days and I was really impressed with it.

It was during the school holidays and my friend, Chris, who also knew nothing about carp fishing, and I had gone to the lake for a few hours' sport. I was using double maggot on a size 14 hook, straight to 5lb main line. The lake was fairly deep, so I was fishing on the drop. After casting and throwing out a couple of handfuls of maggots, I decided to set up my leger rod and was halfway through making this up when some instinct told me to turn round and look at my float rod, just as it was sliding off the rest.

I had never seen a carp in the flesh before, let alone caught one, and as I lifted the rod, it doubled over. I quickly undid the rear drag on the reel, whereupon the reel screamed and the fish, which I thought might be a tench, sped to the other side of the lake, taking about 80 yards of line with it. In retrospect, I now realise that I was lucky to have caught the fish where I did; there was only one serious snag on the lake and that was at the other end.

Being totally ignorant of the laws of big fish, I began to follow it round the lake but fortunately, at this precise moment, one of my school pals, Steve, was walking along the opposite bank. He had been a member of the carp syndicate for a few years and knew a fair bit about the art of carp fishing. As soon as he saw what was happening, he shouted across the lake,

"Stay where you are. Don't follow it!"

Of course, I stayed put and by the time Steve arrived breathlessly at my side, I had managed to regain a large amount of line. If it hadn't been for Steve, I would never have landed it. He talked me through the whole 40 minutes that the fish was on.

It was mid-July and the water level had dropped considerably so, when I did manage to get the fish to the bank, it beached itself about ten feet out. Luckily for me, Steve, and the fish, I was wearing my father's waders and was able to kick them off so that Steve could put them on and go in to scoop the carp into the net.

By this time, there were crowds of people around us and I felt really proud, although I received the evil eye from the 'real' carp anglers who had been camped out all week, but that was understandable; I was only a kid and not even trying! The adrenalin rush was unbelievable and I can remember sitting on the bank, after returning the carp, for at least an hour before I stopped shaking.

Anyway, as I said, this was six years ago and even though I tried to emulate my peers and catch more carp by copying their methods, buying all the right gear and putting as much time as I could in at the lake, I was unsuccessful, so I gave up and turned to tench fishing instead.

It was not until halfway through last season that I returned to carp fishing in a big way. One of my father's friends had been carp fishing for years and he gave me some of his own bait to try out. I was still fishing for tench, but I had stepped up all my gear to 2¼lb rods and 10lb line.

About August last year, to my surprise and delight, I began to catch carp quite regularly, including several 20s. Father's friend gave me all the help I needed regarding rigs and making my own bait, together with advice when I went to buy bite alarms, new rods etc.

This season, I began with a mission. I was determined to catch the same big carp I had caught six years ago but, until 20th September, although I managed to capture 12 double-figure fish from the lake, there was no sign of the big one.

I put in quite a few long sessions, but I think the reason for my success was that I stuck to the same recipe and flavouring of my bait, which I believe in the summer and autumn months definitely gets results.

Most semi-hard waters will produce fish on a bait if it is introduced quite regularly and my bait had been going into the lake at least once or twice a week since the start of the season. It seems that the fish are really feeding well on it and I can almost guarantee at least one carp per session.

Before 20th September, I had put in the odd day on the lake, with average results, so I decided to undertake a night session with my cousin, Paul. It had been raining quite heavily for a couple of days and the water temperature had risen by a few degrees. The conditions were perfect and we had the whole lake to ourselves. The afternoon fishing was very quiet and we couldn't see carp moving anywhere but, around six o'clock, the fish went crazy and began topping all around the margins.

I decided to move both my baits to where I had seen the fish and because there was no one else on the water, I was able to walk one of them to the far bank, about 250 yards. The other bait was placed about six feet out from the bank on my left, where I had already put down about a hundred boilies and a couple of pints of hemp.

During the long wait, my left Delkim kept giving single bleeps every hour or so, so at about 11pm, I thought I'd better check it. A spider had spun a web from my swinger to the alarm and rather than destroy all the poor little devil's hard work, I turned down the sensitivity on this alarm while Paul tried to feed the spider with a handful of crane flies which he was in the process of evicting from his bivvy. The spider seemed grateful.

All evening, Paul had been saying that he was very confident that one of us would catch, but he's hardly ever right in his predictions, so I had different ideas. Usually, when the fish are active, as they were that evening, we would catch quite quickly, as had happened to me on a number of occasions.

The obvious answer was that the carp simply weren't feeding, but other anglers had told me a number of times that the big mirror nearly always emerged when nothing else was feeding. I could only hope.

Paul and I retired to our bivvies at about half past midnight and I went out like a light. At 1.30am, I was woken by four bleeps; I looked out of the door and my left-hand swinger was on the ground. Jumping out of my sleeping bag, I stumbled down the bank and as I reached the rods, the swinger twitched up an inch. I hit it.

The fish was kiting to the right and I still hadn't connected with it. Paul looked out of his bivvy when the alarm had gone off and then crashed out again, thinking I had missed it. I was too busy concentrating on the fish to call him but suddenly, he was up, ready and beside me with the net.

Afterwards, he told me that he had got up was because he heard me talking to myself. Apparently, I kept saying: "It's kiting everywhere!" over and over again. I was totally unaware that I was doing this but, by now, I had caught up with the fish; and the fish had caught up with my other rod.

Everything suddenly became very heavy as my other rod started nodding and the Delkim bleeped its heart out. Paul quickly picked it up and ran with it down the bank to my right. I was a little worried, as he started to reel it in, thinking that he might knock the fish off. I must confess that I didn't know it was the biggie at that moment but, as soon as Paul returned with my rod, tackle and all, it clicked.

What I had on was not a load of other gear. It was a big fish.

While all this was happening, the fish decided to have a rest and just locked solid. Then, without warning, it went berserk. I couldn't backwind fast enough, so I flicked the baitrunner back on as it shot about 100 yards to the middle of the lake into the deep water. It stayed there for about 15 minutes, kiting left and right, with the unmistakable slow nod that most big fish give you in deep water.

My arm was really starting to ache; the fish had been on for 25 minutes so I decided to give it a bit more stick, this time managing to get the fish to the surface, still about 40 yards from the bank. It rolled, made two more last efforts for freedom, and finally gave up. Paul was already up to his waist in the water with the net. As I slowly eased the fish towards him, he gave one quick scoop and the fish was ours. I can remember Paul shouting, "Yes!" as it flopped into the net.

We put the carp on the mat and unhooked it. When I fish at night, I use a red light, as it doesn't seem to spook the fish so much. On this occasion, I wished that I hadn't. The carp weighed 27lb 10oz and as I checked its condition prior to returning it to the water, I found a large sore on its left flank. I was more than a little worried, so I finished off the film in the camera and took it to be developed the next day.

When I collected the photos, I was horrified to see that the carp was covered in a red rash and that it had a fair few sores all over it. The reason I didn't notice this when I checked it out on the bank was because of the red light. Anyone who has worked in, or visited, a photographic dark room will know that under red light, anything red becomes invisible. The flash on the camera, being white light, obviously showed everything up on the photos.

I went straight to the managers of our club and showed them the pictures. They were quite concerned, but explained to me that the fish was well over 40 years old and that things like this often happened to older fish. If I had caught the carp at the start of the season, I wouldn't have been so

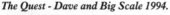

The Quest - Dave and Big Scale 1994.

worried because many fish get scarred in a similar way due to spawning.

Just to be on the safe side, the club managers kept a couple of my snaps and sent them to the NRA laboratory to find out exactly what could be done – if anything. We haven't heard from them yet, but I sincerely hope something can be done. It's just a shame to see such a well-loved carp in that condition and if he dies, it will be like losing an old friend.

Foot in Mouth
Written mid-epidemic 2001

So, what are you all going to do with yourselves with many of the country's waters closed and all those boilies sitting redundantly in cupboards and freezers nationwide? I did a survey of family and friends and heard some spectacular tales of woe brought about because anglers have 'foot in mouth'. They had rashly agreed to help about the house and garden while confined to barracks.

"I've gotta decorate the whole house!" said one particularly grief-stricken carper, "starting with the spare bedroom. What's she want that decorated for? It's a spare room, no one ever goes in there...mutter, grumble, more mutter."

"I dunno what I'm making all this bait for," said another, ankle deep in homemades, "or what I'm going to do with it. The freezer in the garage is full to bursting...I don't suppose you've got any room in yours, Rose...?"

I beat a hasty retreat and continued commiserating with his wife who is going through hell due to a deep depression – not hers, that of her spouse.
"I don't know what all the fuss is about," she said. "Up until a few years ago it would have been the close season, anyway, and they reckon it'll be under control by the summer."

So, when you've done with cleaning rods, taking apart and servicing reels, after having eventually found the bits that have pinged off on to a patterned carpet, made enough rigs to see you through to Armageddon and wandered disconsolately around tackle shops with your hands in your pockets, what then?

You can read all the angling publications from cover to cover, at least twice, disagree with everything Jim Gibbinson says, re-read it, and realise that he was right all along. Wonder how Jules Cundiff manages to keep Kevin Keegan's old hair-cut and still look okay, and marvel at the fact that Tim Paisley's leaders are far more interesting than day-time TV; funny how you'd never noticed before. On the other hand, you could have a go at some of those jobs at home that you've been promising to do for years. You can relate everything to fishing, you know; all it takes is a little imagination.

Think of using a paint-roller as a means to improving the strength in your casting arm, or shingle a pathway by using a throwing stick and one pea shingle at a time. Imagine the accuracy you could achieve! Hoovering is very much like weed raking. Learn to avoid snags by simulating the TV and small items of furniture as potential hazards. Putting the ironing away is much like stacking a bivvy.

I've seen anglers take weeks to carve out a swim from a particularly obstinate clump of bramble but recoil in horror if requested to 'dig up that five yards of garden by the compost heap, for me.' Lawn mowers trigger a similar reaction. Think 'work-party', that's the secret. I know no one likes those either, but they do pay dividends in the end and the same applies to household chores. Imagine the brownie points you can rack up for the future. When the return to the countryside is fully operational, you'll be able to get away with all kinds of stuff which, had you not put in the time and effort, might have taken days of smooth talking, meals out and a bouquet.

The degree of pain that certain anglers of my acquaintance are going through brings a tear to the eye. I know of one party of carpers who are so desperate that they've opted for a trip to Poland. They're prepared to tolerate possible snow and a diet of boiled cabbage for a fortnight, just on the off chance of catching a carp or two.

There are others who have donned heavy disguise, so their dyed-in-the-wool carping mates won't find out, and sneaked off at night on to the high seas - all right, the Thames Estuary but it's close enough - in search of sea species. They professed to have enjoyed catching skate and whiting but you can just tell that their hearts are by a stillwater. It's tragic.

What I'd like to know is why there seem to be no restrictions upon golfers, not in my area, anyway. Quite a few golf courses back on to farmland but we don't hear of them closing their doors to the punters. I bet golf widows don't have to go through all manner of mood swings and fits of weeping into pint glasses because their men can't follow their greatest passion in life.

Bear up, girls. It'll all be over by Christmas.